Indonesian
phrase book

Berlitz Publishing Company, Inc.

Princeton   Mexico City   London   Eschborn   Singapore

Berlitz Trademark Reg. US Patent Office and other countries
Marca Registrada

Cover photo: © Berlitz – photo by Pete Bennett
ISBN 2-8315-7092-1
Third printing - July 2001
Printed in Spain

Developed and produced for Berlitz Publishing Company by
G&W Publishing Services, Oxfordshire, U.K.

Indonesian edition: Katrina Hayward and Dr. Brian Smith

Contents

Pronunciation

This section is designed to make you familiar with the sounds of Indonesian by using our simplified phonetic transcription. You'll find the pronunciation of the Indonesian letters and sounds explained below, together with their "imitated" equivalents. This system is used throughout the phrase book: simply read the pronunciation as if it were English, noting any special rules below.

In this phrase book we have used a friendly system to achieve a close approximation of the pronunciation, although this inevitably means some simplification of the more subtle aspects of Indonesian pronunciation.

The Indonesian language

The national language is Bahasa Indonesia, which is spoken by most Indonesians as well as their own regional language. Indonesian and Malay are very similar languages. Indeed, after years of negotiation, in 1972 the two countries agreed on a standard spelling to be used in both countries.

The pronunciation of Indonesian and Malay varies in the same way as British and American English do. Most of the vocabulary is common to both languages but there are a few differences.

While Indonesian has many words that come from Dutch, the former colonial power, Malay – a former British colony – has a similar number of words that come from English. For example, the word for 'office' in Indonesian is **kantor**, whereas Malay uses the English-sounding **ofis**. Both languages also have a large number of words of Arabic origin, dating from an earlier period.

A feature of Indonesian is its use of prefixes and suffixes which are attached to a large number of words (see page 169). While the root word is understood and often used in colloquial speech, affixes are often added in more formal speech and in writing.

Regional languages

There are more than 300 languages spoken throughout
Indonesia. Except for those in the northern island of
Halmahera and most of Irian Jaya, these languages
belong to the Malay-Polynesian group. Within this
group there are many different regional languages and dialects.

Pronunciation

The sounds of Indonesian are reasonably accessible to English
speakers. Indonesian is generally spelled as it sounds and it is
quite easy to speak Indonesian reasonably well. There are slight
regional variations in pronunciation but English-speaking
learners usually find it easy to make themselves understood.
A short description of the spelling and sounds of Indonesian
is given below.

Consonants

Letter	Description of sound	Example	Symbol	Pronunciation
b,d,f,j,l,m n,p,s,v,w	are pronounced approximately as in English			
c	like *ch* in *child*	**capai** (tired)	*ch*	*chapay*
		cinta (love)		
h	like *h* in *hot*, except at the end of a word where it is hardly noticeable	**hakim** (judge)	*h*	*hakim*
		boleh (can)	–	*bole*
		sudah (already)	–	*suda*
k	like English *c* in *cut* except at the end of a word, where it sounds more like the *k* in *skin*	**kota** (city)	*c*	*cota*
		kotak (box)	*k*	*cotak*
kh	like *ch* in Scottish *loch*	**khas** (special)	*kh*	*chas*
ng/ngg	like *ng* in *singer*	**datang** (come)	*ng*	*datang*
		bangun (wake)	*ngg*	*banggun*
ny	like *ny* in *canyon*	**nyonya** (Miss)	*ny*	*nyonya*

| r | usually trilled like a Spanish (Scottish) *r* | **roti** (bread) | *r* | *rotee* |
| **y** | like *y* in *yes* | **saya** (I, me) | *y* | *saya* |

Vowels

a	like *u* in *cup*; pronounced as two '*a*'s with a gap between	**anak** (child) **maaf** (sorry)	*a* *a'a*	*anak* *ma'af*
e	1) like *e* in *met* 2) like *a* in *alone* in unstressed syllables	**sate** (sate) **empat** (four)	*e* *er*	*sate* *ermpat*
i	1) like *i* in *it* 2) like *ee* in *see*	**sakit** (ill) **ibu** (mother)	*i* *ee*	*sakit* *eeboo*
o	like *o* in *ox*	**orang** (person) **boleh** (may)	*o*	*orang* *bole*
u	1) like *oo* in *book* in closed syllables 2) like *oo* in *boot* in open syllables	**tutup** (shut) **satu** (one)	*u* *oo*	*tutup* *satoo*

Diphthongs

| **ai** | like *ie* in *pie*, except at the end of a word where it is like *ay* in *say* | **naik** (go up) **capai** (tired) | *ai* *ay* | *naik* *chapay* |
| **au** | like *ow* in *cow* | **laut** (sea) | *ow* | *lowt* |

8

Stress

The stress in Indonesian usually falls on the second to last syllable, e.g. **bukan** (not), **beberapa** (several). However, if the vowel of the second to last syllable is the neutral **e** (written in the phonetics in this book as *er*), the stress usually falls on the last syllable, e.g. **belum** (not yet).

Pronunciation of the Indonesian alphabet

A	*a*		**N**	*en*
B	*be*		**O**	*o*
C	*che*		**P**	*pe*
D	*de*		**Q**	*kee*
E	*e*		**R**	*er*
F	*ef*		**S**	*es*
G	*ge*		**T**	*te*
H	*ha*		**U**	*oo*
I	*ee*		**V**	*fe*
J	*ye*		**W**	*we*
K	*ka*		**X**	*ecs*
L	*el*		**Y**	*ye*
M	*em*		**Z**	*zet*

Basic Expressions

ESSENTIAL

Yes.	**Ya.** *ya*
No.	**Tidak.** *tidak*
Okay.	**Baik.** *baik*
Please.	**Tolong.** *tolong*
Thank you.	**Terima kasih.** *terrima casi*
Thank you very much.	**Terima kasih banyak.** *terrima casi banyak*

Greetings/Apologies
Ucapan selamat/Permohonan maaf

Hello./Hi!	**Halo./Hai!** *halo/hai*
Good morning/afternoon.	**Selamat pagi/siang.** *serlamat pagee/siang*
Good evening/night.	**Selamat sore/malam.** *serlamat sore/malam*
Good-bye.	**Sampai jumpa.** *sampay jumpa*
Excuse me! (*getting attention*)	**Permisi!** *permisee*
Excuse me!/Sorry!	**Maaf!** *ma'af*
Don't mention it.	**Tidak apa-apa.** *tidak apa apa*

Communication difficulties
Kesulitan berkomunikasi

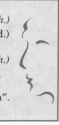

Do you speak English?

Apakah anda bisa berbahasa Inggris?
apaca anda bisa berbahasa ingrees

Could you speak more slowly?

Bisa anda berbicara lebih pelan?
bisa anda berbichara lerbih perlan

Could you repeat that?

Bisa anda ulang lagi?
bisa anda oolang lagee

Excuse me? [Pardon?]

Maaf? *ma'af*

What was that?

Apa itu tadi? *apa itoo tadee*

Could you spell it?

Bisa anda mengeja?
bisa anda merngeja

Please write it down.

Tolong dituliskan.
tolong deetooleescan

Can you translate this for me?

Bisa anda terjemahkan untuk saya?
bisa anda terjemakan untuk saya

What does this/that mean?

Apa artinya ini/itu?
apaca artinya inee/itoo

Please point to the phrase in the book.

Tolong tunjukkan kalimat itu di buku.
tolong tunjuccan itoo dee bucoo

I understand.

Saya mengerti *saya merngerti*

I don't understand.

Saya tidak mengerti
saya tidak merngerti

– Semuanya lima ribu tiga ratus rupiah.
(That's five thousand and three hundred rupiah.)
– Saya tidak mengerti. (I don't understand.)
– Semuanya lima ribu tiga ratus rupiah.
(That's five thousand and three hundred rupiah.)
Tolong dituliskan. ... Ah, "5,300 rupiah".
Nah ini ya.
(Please write it down. ... Ah, "5,300 rupiah".
Here you are.)

Questions Pertanyaan-pertanyaan

GRAMMAR

Questions may be asked in Indonesian in several ways:
1. by using rising intonation – **Dia sakit?** (She's sick?)
2. by using **-kah** (commonly in writing or formal speech) – **Sakitkah dia?** (Is she sick?)
3. by using **apa** or **apakah** – **Apa dia sudah pergi?** (Has he gone?)
4. by using a question word, e.g. **siapa** (who), **berapa** (how much/many), etc. – **Berapa harganya?** (How much does it cost?)

Where? Dimana?

Where is it?	**Dimana itu?** *dimana itoo*
Where are you going?	**Kemana anda mau pergi?** *cermana anda mow pergee*
across the road	**ke seberang jalan** *cer serberang jalan*
around the town	**keliling kota** *cerleeling cota*
at the meeting place [point]	**di tempat pertemuan** *di termpat pertermooan*
from the U.S.	**dari Amerika Serikat** *daree america serreecat*
here/there	**di sini/di sana** *dee sinee/dee sana*
in Indonesia	**di Indonesia** *dee indonesia*
in the car	**di dalam mobil** *dee dalam mobil*
inside	**di dalam** *dee dalam*
near the bank	**dekat bank** *decat bank*
next to the post office	**disebelah kantor pos** *deeserberlah cantor pos*
opposite the market	**diseberang pasar** *diserberrang pasar*
on the left/right	**disebelah kiri/kanan** *deeserberlah ciree/canan*
on the sidewalk [pavement]	**di tepi jalan** *dee terpee jalan*
outside the café	**di luar kafe** *dee looar cafe*
to the hotel	**ke hotel** *cer hotel*
towards Jakarta	**ke arah Jakarta** *cer arah jakarta*

When? Kapan?

When does the train arrive? **Jam berapa kereta tiba?**
jam berrapa cereta teeba

When does the museum open? **Jam berapa museum dibuka?** *jam berrapa museum dibooca*

after lunch **setelah makan siang** *sertelah macan siang*

always **selalu** *serlaloo*

around midnight **sekitar tengah malam** *sercitar tengah malam*

at 7 o'clock **pada jam tujuh** *pada jam tujuh*

before Friday **sebelum hari Jum'at** *serbelum haree juma'at*

by tomorrow **besok** *besok*

every week **setiap minggu** *sertiap mingoo*

for 2 hours **selama dua jam** *serlama dooa jam*

from 9 a.m. to 6 p.m. **dari jam sembilan pagi sampai jam enam malam** *daree jam sermbilan pagee sampay jam malam*

in 20 minutes **dalam waktu duapuluh menit** *dalam wactoo dooapuluh mernit*

never **tidak pernah** *tidak pernah*

not yet **belum** *berlum*

now **sekarang** *sercarang*

often **sering** *serring*

on March 8 **pada tanggal delapan Maret** *pada tangal derlapan maret*

on weekdays **pada hari kerja** *pada haree cerja*

sometimes **kadang-kadang** *cadang cadang*

soon **segera** *sergerra*

then **dulu** *dooloo*

10 minutes ago **sepuluh menit lalu** *serpeluh mernit laloo*

What kind of …? … yang seperti apa?

This is/That is …	**Ini/Itu …**	_inee/itoo_
beautiful/ugly	**bagus/jelek**	_bagus/jerlek_
better/worse	**lebih baik/lebih buruk**	_lerbih baik/lerbih buruk_
big/small	**besar/kecil**	_bersar/cerchil_
cheap/expensive	**murah/mahal**	_murah/mahal_
clean/dirty	**bersih/kotor**	_bersih/cotor_
dark/light	**gelap/terang**	_gerlap/terrang_
delicious/revolting	**enak/tidak enak**	_enak/tidak enak_
early/late	**terlalu awal/terlambat**	_terlaloo awal/terlambat_
easy/difficult	**mudah/sukar**	_mudah/sukar_
empty/full	**kosong/penuh**	_cosong/pernuh_
good/bad	**baik/buruk**	_baik/buruk_
heavy/light	**berat/ringan**	_berat/ringan_
hot/warm/cold	**panas/hangat/dingin**	_panas/hangat/dingin_
narrow/wide	**sempit/luas**	_sermpit/luas_
next/last	**yang berikut/yang lalu**	_yang bericut/yang laloo_
old/new	**lama/baru**	_lama/baroo_
open/shut	**buka/tutup**	_buca/tutup_
pleasant/unpleasant	**menyenangkan/tidak menyenangkan**	_mernyernangkan/tidak mernyernangkan_
quick/slow	**cepat/lambat**	_cerpat/lambat_
quiet/noisy	**tenang/ribut**	_ternang/ribut_
right/wrong	**benar/salah**	_bernar/salah_
tall/short	**tinggi/pendek**	_tingee/pendek_
thick/thin	**tebal/tipis**	_terbal/tipis_
vacant/occupied	**kosong/terisi**	_cosong/terisee_
young/old	**muda/tua**	_muda/tua_

In Indonesian, nouns have no articles (*a/an* and *the*)
and there is often no difference between singular
and plural nouns.
Plural meaning is sometimes conveyed by doubling the
noun, e.g. **anak** (child) → **anak-anak** (children).

How much/many? Berapa banyak?

How much is that?	**Berapa harga itu?** *berrapa harga itoo*
How many are there?	**Ada berapa banyak?** *ada berrapa banyak*
1/2/3	**satu/dua/tiga** *satoo/dua/tiga*
4/5	**empat/lima** *ermpat/lima*
none	**tidak ada** *tidak ada*
about 100 rupiah	**sekitar seratus rupiah** *sercitar serratus rupia*
a little/a lot (of)	**sedikit/banyak** *serdikit/banyak*
enough	**cukup** *chukup*
few/a few of them	**beberapa/sebagian dari mereka** *berberrapa/serbagian daree merreka*
more than that	**lebih dari itu** *lerbih daree itoo*
less than that	**kurang dari itu** *kurang daree itoo*
much more	**lebih banyak lagi** *lerbih banyak lagee*
nothing else	**tidak ada lagi** *tidak ada lagee*
too much	**terlalu banyak** *terlaloo banyak*

Why? Mengapa?

Why is that?	**Mengapa demikian?** *merngapa dermician*
Why not?	**Mengapa tidak?** *merngapa tidak*
I don't know why.	**Saya tidak tahu mengapa.** *saya tidak tahoo merngapa*

15

Who?/Which? Siapa?/Yang mana?

Who's there?	**Siapa itu?**	*siapa itoo*
Who is it for?	**Untuk siapa itu?**	*untuk siapa itoo*
(for) her/him	**(untuk) dia**	*(untuk) dia*
(for) me	**(untuk) saya**	*(untuk) saya*
(for) you	**(untuk) anda**	*(untuk) anda*
(for) them	**(untuk) mereka**	*(untuk) merreka*
someone	**seseorang**	*serserorang*
no one	**tidak siapapun**	*tidak siapapun*
Which one do you want?	**Yang mana yang anda mau?**	*yang mana yang anda mow*
this one/that one	**yang ini/yang itu**	*yang inee/yang itoo*
one like that	**yang seperti itu**	*yang serperti itoo*
not that one	**bukan yang itu**	*bucan yang itoo*
something	**sesuatu**	*sersuatoo*
nothing	**tidak ada apa-apa**	*tidak ada apa apa*

Whose? Siapa punya?

Whose is that?	**Siapa punya itu?**	*siapa punya itoo*
That's …	**Itu …**	*itoo*
mine/ours/yours	**milik saya/milik kami/milik anda**	*milik saya/milik camee/milik anda*
his/hers/theirs	**milik dia/milik dia/milik mereka**	*milik dia/milik dia/milik merreca*
It's … turn.	**Sekarang giliran …**	*sercarang giliran*
my/our/your	**saya/kami/anda**	*saya/camee/anda*
his/her/their	**dia/dia/mereka**	*dia/dia/merreca*

GRAMMAR

The personal pronouns – **saya** (I), **anda** (you), **dia** (he/she/it), **kami** (we), **mereka** (they) – are also used as possessive adjectives but, like other adjectives, they *follow* the noun, e.g. **anak saya** (my child).

How? Bagaimana?

How would you like to pay?	**Apakah anda bayar kontan atau dengan kartu kredit?** _apaca anda bayar contan atow dengan cartu credit_
by cash	**kontan** _contan_
by credit card	**dengan kartu kredit** _dengan cartu credit_
How are you getting here?	**Bagaimana caranya anda sampai kesini?** _bagaimana charanya anda sampai cersinee_
by car/bus/train	**dengan mobil/bis/kereta** _dengan mobil/bis/cerreta_
on foot	**jalan kaki** _jalan cacee_

Is it …?/Are there …? Apakah ini …?

Is it free of charge?	**Apakah ini gratis?** _apaca inee gratis_
It isn't ready.	**Belum selesai.** _berlum serlesai_
Is there a shower in the room?	**Apakah di kamar ada pancuran mandi?** _apaca dee camar ada panchuran mandee_
Are there any buses into town?	**Apakah ada bis yang ke pusat kota?** _apaca ada bis yang cer pusat cota_
There it is/they are.	**Nah, itu dia.** _na itoo dia_
Are there buses into town?	**Apakah ada banyak yang bis ke kota?** _apaca ada banyak yang bis cer cota_
There aren't any towels in my room.	**Tidak ada handuk di kamar saya.** _tidak ada handuk dee camar saya_
Here it is/they are.	**Nah, ini dia.** _na inee dia_
There it is/they are.	**Nah, itu dia.** _na itoo dia_

Can/May? Bisa/Boleh?

Can I …?	**Bisa saya …?** _bisa saya_
May we …?	**Boleh kami …?** _bole camee_
Can you show me …?	**Bisa anda tunjukkan saya …?** _bisa anda tunjuccan saya_
Can you tell me …?	**Bisa anda jelaskan saya …?** _bisa anda jerlascan saya_
May I help you?	**Boleh saya bantu?** _bole saya bantoo_
Can you direct me to …?	**Bisa anda tunjukkan saya jalan ke …?** _bisa anda tunjuccan saya jalan ce_
I can't.	**Saya tidak bisa.** _saya tidak bisa_

What do you want?
Apa yang anda inginkan

I'd like …	**Saya mau …** _saya mow_
Could I have …?	**Bisa saya dapat …?** _bisa saya dapat_
We'd like …	**Kami mau …** _camee mow_
Give me …	**Berikan saya …** _berrican saya_
I'm looking for …	**Saya cari …** _saya charee_
I need to …	**Saya perlu …** _saya perloo_
go/find …	**pergi/cari …** _pergee/charee_
see …	**bertemu …** _bertermoo_
speak to …	**berbicara dengan …** _berbichara dengan_

> – Permisi. (Excuse me.)
> – _Ya? Bisa saya bantu? (Yes? Can I help you?)_
> – Bisa saya berbicara dengan Bapak Santoso?
>   (Can I speak to Bapak Santoso?)
> – _Mohon tunggu sebentar. (Just a moment, please.)_

18

Other useful words
Kata-kata berguna lainnya

fortunately	**untungnya** _untungnya_
hopefully	**mudah-mudahan** _mudah mudahan_
of course	**tentu saja** _tentu saja_
perhaps	**barangkali** _barangkalee_
unfortunately	**sayangnya** _sayangnya_
also/but	**juga/tapi** _juga/tapee_
and/or	**dan/atau** _dan/atow_

Exclamations Kata Seru

At last!	**Akhirnya!** _akhirnya_
Go on.	**Ayo.** _ayo_
Nonsense!	**Omong kosong!** _omong cosong_
That's true.	**Itu benar.** _itoo bernar_
No way!	**Tidak mungkin!** _tidak mungkin_
How are things?	**Bagaimana kabarnya?** _bagaimana cabarnya_
very good	**baik sekali** _baik secalee_
fine	**baik** _baik_
not bad	**lumayan** _lumayan_
okay	**baik** _baik_
not good	**kurang baik** _curang baik_
fairly bad	**cukup buruk** _chucup buruk_
terrible	**sangat buruk** _sangat buruk_

Accommodations

Hotels come in different grades of price and comfort. All hotels are required to pay a government tax of 10 percent. This may be passed on to the customer, but most cheap hotels either absorb the tax into their room rates or avoid it. Some mid-range and top hotels charge a 21 percent tax and service charge.

Penginapan/Losmen
At the bottom end of the scale, spartan with shared bathrooms. Many are good family-run establishments, but others can be of very poor quality.

Wisma
These are slightly more up-scale, but still cheap.

Hotels
These are divided into two grades: **melati** or **yasmin**, 'flower' grades which indicate hotels of a relatively low standard; and **bintang** (star) hotels which are more luxurious. A hotel at the bottom of the range is **satu melati** (one melati) while at the top end a five-star hotel is **bintang lima**.

Mid-range hotels usually come with a private bath. Five-star hotels match those in the west and often quote prices in US dollars.

The cost of accommodations varies considerably across the archipelago – the out-of-the-way places being more expensive. Bali has the widest range and the best standards but prices in the main resorts for mid- and top-range hotels are high.

Reservations Penempahan tempat

In advance Dimuka

Can you recommend a
hotel in …?

**Tahu anda hotel yang
cukup baik di …?**
*tahu anda hotel yang chucup
baik dee*

How much is it per night?

Berapa harganya per malam?
berrapa harganya per malam

Do you have a
cheaper room?

Apa ada kamar yang lebih murah?
apaca ada camar yang lerbi mura

Could you reserve me a
room there, please?

**Bisa tolong pesankan kamar untuk
saya disana?** *bisa tolong persankan
camar untuk saya disana*

How do I get there?

Bagaimana caranya saya kesana?
bagaimana charanya saya cersana

At the hotel Di hotel

Do you have a room?

Apakah ada kamar kosong?
apaca ada camar cosong

I'd like a room with …

Saya mau kamar yang ada …
saya mow camar yang ada

twin beds

dua tempat tidur *dua termpat tidur*

a double bed

**satu tempat tidur besar untuk dua
orang** *satoo termpat tidur bersar
untuk dua orang*

a bath/shower

**bak untuk berendam/pancuran
mandi** *bak untuk berrendam/
panchuran mandee*

– Apakah ada kamar kosong?
(Do you have a room?)
– Maaf, kami penuh. (I'm sorry, we're full.)
– Oh. Apakah ada hotel lain di dekat sini?
(Oh. Is there another hotel nearby?)
– Ya bu/pak. The Hotel Ambassador sangat dekat.
(Yes, madam/sir. The Hotel Ambassador is very near.)

Reception Resepsi

I have a reservation.
Saya sudah pesan kamar. *saya suda pesan camar*

My name is …
Nama saya … *nama saya*

We've reserved a double and a single room.
Kami sudah pesan satu kamar untuk dua orang dan satu kamar untuk satu orang. *camee suda pesan satoo camar untuk dua orang dan satoo camar untuk satoo orang*

I confirmed my reservation by mail.
Saya sudah pastikan pemesanan kamar saya lewat surat. *saya suda pastikan permesanan camar saya lewat surat*

Amenities and facilities Sarana dan fasilitas

Is there (a) … in the room?
Apakah ada … dalam kamar? *apaca ada … dalam camar*

air conditioning
AC *ase*

TV/telephone
TV/telepon *tivee/telepon*

Does the hotel have (a) …?
Apakah di hotel ini ada …? *apaka dee hotel inee ada*

fax
faks *facs*

satellite TV
TV satelit *tivee satelit*

laundry service
layanan penatu *layanan pernatoo*

sauna/swimming pool
sauna/kolam renang *sowna/colam rernang*

Could you put … in the room?
Bisa dibawakan … ke kamar? *bisa dibawakan … cer camar*

an extra bed
tempat tidur tambahan *termpat tidur tambahan*

a crib [child's cot]
tempat tidur bayi *termpat tidur bayee*

Do you have facilities for children/the disabled?
Apakah ada fasilitas untuk anak-anak /orang cacad *apaca ada fasilitas untuk anak anak/orang chachad*

How long? Berapa lama?

We'll be staying ...	**Kami akan tinggal ...** _camee akan tinggal_
overnight only	**semalam saja** _sermalam saja_
a few days	**beberapa hari** _berberapa haree_
a week (at least)	**satu minggu (paling sedikit)** _satoo minggoo (paling serdikit)_
I'd like to stay an extra night.	**Saya mau tinggal satu malam lagi.** _saya mow tinggal satoo malam lagee_

– Halo, Saya sudah memesan kamar.
Nama saya John Newton.
(Hello, I have a reservation.
My name's John Newton.)
– _Halo Pak Newton._ (Hello. Mr. Newton.)
– Kami sudah memesan kamar untuk dua malam.
(I've reserved a room for two nights.)
– _Baik. Tolong formulir pendaftaran ini diisi._
(OK. Please fill out this registration form.)

May I see your passport, please?	**Boleh saya lihat paspor anda?**
Please fill out this form/ sign here.	**Tolong formulir ini diisi/ tanda tangan disini.**

KAMAR SAJA ... Rp. 50.000	room only ... rp. 50.000
TERMASUK MAKAN PAGI	breakfast included
MAKANAN TERSEDIA	meals available
NAMA KELUARGA/ NAMA DEPAN	last name/first name
ALAMAT RUMAH/JALAN/ NOMOR	home address/street/ number
KEBANGSAAN/PEKERJAAN	nationality/profession
TANGGAL/TEMPAT LAHIR	date/place of birth
NOMOR PASPOR	passport number
TANDA TANGAN	signature

Price Harga

How much is it?	**Berapa harganya?** *berrapa harganya*
per night/week	**per malam/minggu** *per malam/minggoo*
for bed and breakfast	**untuk tempat tidur dan makan pagi** *untuk termpat tidur dan macan pagee*
for American Plan (A.P.) [full board]	**termasuk makan pagi, siang, dan malam** *termasuk macan pagee, siang, danmalam*
for Modified American Plan (M.A.P.) [half board]	**termasuk makan pagi dan malam** *termasuk macan pagee*
Does the price include …?	**Apakah harga ini termasuk …?** *apaca harga inee termasuk*
breakfast	**makan pagi** *macan pagee*
sales tax [VAT]	**Pajak Pertambahan Nilai (PPN)** *pajak pertambahan nilay*
Do I have to pay a deposit?	**Apakah saya harus bayar uang muka?** *apaca saya harus bayar uang muca*
Is there a reduction for children?	**Apakah ada potongan harga untuk anak-anak?** *apaca ada potongan harga untuk anak anak*

Decisions Keputusan-keputusan

May I see the room?	**Boleh saya lihat kamar?** *bole saya lihat camar*
That's fine. I'll take it.	**Ini baik. Saya ambil.** *inee baik. saya ambil*
It's too … dark/small/noisy	**Agak terlalu …** *agak terlaloo* **gelap/kecil/ribut** *gerlap/cerchil/ribut*
Do you have anything bigger/cheaper?	**Apakah ada yang lebih besar/ lebih murah?** *apaca ada yang lebi bersar/lebi mura*
No, I won't take it.	**Tidak, saya tidak mau ambil itu.** *tidak, saya tidak mow ambil itoo*

Problems Masalah-masalah

The … doesn't work.	**… tidak jalan.** *… tidak jalan*
fan	**kipas angin** *cipas angin*
heat	**mesin penghangat** *mesin penghangat*
light	**lampu** *lampoo*
I can't turn the air conditioning on/off.	**Saya tidak bisa menyalakan/ mematikan AC.** *saya tidak bisa nyalakan/matikan ase*
There is no hot water/ toilet paper.	**Tidak ada air panas/kertas toilet.** *tidak ada air panas/certas toilet*
The faucet [tap] is dripping.	**Keran bocor.** *kerran bochor*
The sink/toilet is blocked.	**Bak cuci/toilet tersumbat.** *bak chuchee/toilet tersumbat*
The window/door is jammed.	**Jendela/pintu macet.** *jendela/pintu machet*
My room has not been made up.	**Kamar saya belum dibersihkan.** *kamar saya berlum dibersikan*
The … is/are broken.	**… rusak.** *… rusak*
blinds/shutters	**kerai/daun jendela** *ceray/down jendela*
lamp/lock	**lampu/kunci** *lampoo/kunchee*
There are insects in our room.	**Ada serangga di kamar kami.** *ada serrangga dee kamar kamee*

Action Tindakan

Could you have that taken care of?	**Bisa anda kirim seseorang untuk perbaikinya?** *bisa anda cirim serseorang untuk perbaikinya*
I'd like to move to another room.	**Saya mau pindah ke kamar lain.** *saya mow pinda ce camar lain*
I'd like to speak to the manager.	**Saya mau berbicara dengan manajer.** *saya mow berbichara dengan manajer*

Requirements Keperluan

In the hotel Mengenai hotel

Where's the …?	**Dimana …?** _dimanaka_
bar	**bar** _bar_
dining room	**ruang makan** _ruang macan_
elevator [lift]	**lift** _lift_
parking lot [car park]	**tempat parkir** _termpat parcir_
restroom [toilet]	**kamar kecil** _camar cerchil_
shower room	**kamar mandi** _kamar mandee_
swimming pool	**kolam renang** _colam rernang_
tour operator's bulletin board	**papan pengumuman agen per jalanan** _papan perngumuman agen perjalanan_
Does the hotel have a garage?	**Apakah hotel ini punya garasi?** _apaca hotel inee punya garasee_
Can I use this adapter here?	**Bisa saya memakai adaptor ini disini?** _bisa saya mermakay adaptor disinee_

HANYA UNTUK ALAT PENCUKUR	razors [shavers] only
PINTU DARURAT	emergency exit
PINTU KEBAKARAN	fire door
JANGAN MENGGANGGU	do not disturb
PUTAR … UNTUK SALURAN KELUAR	dial … for an outside line
PUTAR … UNTUK RESEPSI	dial … for reception
JANGAN MEMBAWA HANDUK KE LUAR KAMAR	don't remove towels from the room

Personal needs Kebutuhan pribadi

The key to room …, please.	**Tolong kunci untuk kamar …** _tolong cunchee untuk camar_
I've lost my key.	**Saya kehilangan kunci saya.** _saya kerhilangan cunchee saya_
I've locked myself out of my room.	**Kunci saya tertinggal di dalam kamar.** _cunchee saya tertinggal dee dalam camar_
Could you wake me at …?	**Bisa anda bangunkan saya jam …?** _bisa anda bangunkan saya jam_
I'd like breakfast in my room.	**Saya mau makan pagi di kamar saya.** _saya mow macan pagee dee camar saya_
Can I leave this in the safe?	**Bisa saya titip ini di tempat di kotak penitipan?** _bisa saya titip inee dee kotak pernitipan_
Could I have my things from the safe?	**Bisa saya ambil barang-barang saya dari kotak penitipan?** _bisa saya ambil barang barang saya daree cotak pernitipan_
Where can I find (a) …?	**Dimana saya bisa mencari …?** _dimana saya bisa merncharee_
maid/our tour guide	**pembantu/pemandu wisata kami** _permbantoo/permandoo wisata camee_
May I have (an) extra …?	**Bolehkan kami mendapatkan tambahan …?** _bolekan camee dapatkan tambahan_
bath towel	**handuk mandi** _handuk mandee_
blanket/pillow	**selimut/bantal** _serlimut/bantal_
hangers	**gantungan baju** _gantungan bajoo_
soap	**sabun** _sabun_
Is/Are there any mail/ messages for me?	**Apakah ada surat/pesan untuk saya?** _apaca ada surat/pesan untuk saya_

BREAKFAST ➤ 43; CHANGING MONEY ➤ 138

Renting Penyewaan

We've reserved an apartment/ cottage …	**Kami sudah pesan satu apartemen/ cottage …** _camee suda pesan satoo apartermen/cottage_
in the name of …	**atas nama …** _atas nama_
Where do we pick up the keys?	**Dimana bisa kami ambil kunci?** _dimanaka bisa kamee ambil kunchi_
Where is the…?	**Dimana …?** _dimana_
electric meter/fuse box	**meteran listrik/kotak sekering** _meteran listrik/cotak secering_
valve [stopcock]/ water heater	**katup penutup/mesin pemanas air** _catup pernutup/mesin permanas air_
Are there any spare …?	**Apakah ada ekstra …?** _apaca ada ecstra_
fuses/gas bottles	**sekering/botol gas** _secering/botol gas_
sheets	**seperai** _serperai_
Which day does the maid come?	**Pada hari apa pembantu datang?** _pada haree apa pembantu datang_
When do I put out the trash [rubbish]?	**Kapan sampah diambil?** _kapan sampa diambil_

Problems Masalah-masalah

Where can I contact you?	**Dimana saya bisa hubungi anda?** _dimana saya bisa hubungee anda_
How does the stove [cooker]/water heater work?	**Bagaimana cara menjalankan kompor/mesin pemanas air?** _bagaimana chara jalankan compor/ mesin permanas air_
The … is/are dirty.	**… kotor.** _… cotor_
The … has broken down.	**… rusak.** _… rusak_
We accidentally broke/ lost …	**Kami tidak sengaja telah merusak/ kehilangan …** _camee tidak serngaja tela merrusak/cerhilangan_

Useful terms Kata-kata berguna

dishes [crockery]	**sendok garpu** _sendok/garpoo_
freezer	**lemari pembeku** _lermari permbeku_
frying pan	**panci penggorengan** _panchee pernggorengan_
kettle	**ceret** _cheret_
lamp	**lampu** _lampoo_
refrigerator	**lemari es** _lermari es_
saucepan	**panci** _panchee_
stove [cooker]	**kompor** _compor_
utensils [cutlery]	**peralatan dapur** _perralatan dapur_
washing machine	**mesin cuci** _mesin chuchee_

Rooms kamar

balcony	**teras** _terras_
bathroom	**kamar mandi** _camar mandee_
bedroom	**kamar tidur** _camar tidur_
dining room	**ruang makan** _ruang macan_
kitchen	**dapur** _dapur_
living room	**ruang keluarga** _ruang cerluarga_
toilet	**kamar kecil** _camar cerchil_

Youth hostel Wisma pemuda (Youth hostel)

Do you have any places left for tonight?	**Apakah anda punya tempat untuk malam ini?** _apaca anda punya termpat untuk malam ini_
Do you rent bedding?	**Apakah anda sewakan peralatan tidur?** _apaca anda sewakan perralatan tidur_
I have an International Student Card.	**Saya punya kartu mahasiswa internasional.** _saya punya cartoo mahasiswa internasional_

REQUIREMENTS ➤ 26; CAMPING ➤ 30

Camping Berkemah

Reservations Pemesanan tempat

Is there a camp site near here?
Apakah ada tempat berkemah dekat sini? _apaca ada termpat berkemah dekat sinee_

Do you have space for a tent/trailer [caravan]?
Apakah ada tempat untuk tenda/karavan? _apaca ada termpat untuk tenda/caravan_

What is the charge …?
Berapa biayanya …? _berrapa biayanya_

per day/week
per hari/minggu _per haree/minggoo_

for a tent/car
untuk satu tenda/mobil _untuk satoo tenda/mobil_

for a trailer [caravan]
untuk satu karavan _untuk satoo caravan_

Facilities Fasilitas

Are there cooking facilities on site?
Apakah ada fasilitas memasak di lokasi? _apaca ada fasilitas mermasak dee locasee_

Are there any electrical outlets [power points]?
Apakah ada stop kontak? _apaca ada stop contak_

Where is/are the …?
Dimana …? _dimana_

drinking water
air minum _air minum_

trash cans [dustbins]
tempat sampah _termpat sampa_

laundry facilities
tempat mencuci pakaian _termpat mernchuchee pacaian_

showers
pancuran mandi _panchuran mandee_

Where can I get some butane gas?
Dimana bisa saya membeli gas? _dimana bisa saya mermbelee gas_

DILARANG BERKEMAH	no camping
AIR MINUM	drinking water
DILARANG MENYALAKAN API UNGGUN	no fires/barbecues

Complaints Keluhan-keluhan

It's too sunny here. | **Di sini terlalu terik.**
dee sinee terlaloo terrik

It's too shady/crowded here. | **Di sini terlalu rindang/ ramai.** *dee sinee terlaloo rindang/ramay*

The ground's too hard/ uneven. | **Tanah terlalu keras/tidak rata.**
tana terlaloo cerras/tidak rata

Do you have a more level spot? | **Apakah ada tempat yang lebih rata permukaannya?** *apaca ada termpat yang lebi rata permukaannya*

Camping equipment Peralatan kemah

butane gas	**gas** *gas*
charcoal	**arang** *arang*
flashlight [torch]	**lampu senter** *lampoo senter*
groundcloth [groundsheet]	**alas tanah** *alas tana*
guy rope	**tali rami** *talee ramee*
hammer	**palu** *paloo*
kerosene [primus] stove	**kompor minyak tanah** *compor minyak tana*
knapsack	**ransel** *ransel*
mallet	**martil kayu** *martil cayoo*
matches	**korek api** *corek apee*
(air) mattress	**matras** *matras*
paraffin	**lilin** *lilin*
sleeping bag	**kantung tidur** *cantung tidur*
tent	**tenda** *tenda*
tent pegs	**pasak tenda** *pasak tenda*
tent pole	**tiang tenda** *tiang tenda*

Checking out lapor keluar

What time do we have to check out? | **Jam berapa kami harus keluar?** *jam berrapa camee harus cerluar*

Could we leave our baggage here until ... p.m.? | **Bisa kami titip koper kami disini sampai jam ...?** *bisa camee titip coper disinee sampay jam*

I'm leaving now. | **Saya mau berangkat sekarang.** *saya mow berrangkat sercarang*

Could you call me a taxi, please? | **Bisa tolong pesankan taksi untuk saya?** *bisa tolong persancan tacsee untuk saya*

It's been a very enjoyable stay. | **Sangat menyenangkan menginap disini.** *sangat mernyenangcan merginap disinee*

Paying Pembayaran

May I have my bill, please? | **Boleh saya minta bon?** *bole saya minta bon*

How much is my telephone bill? | **Berapa bon telepon?** *berrapa bon telepon*

I think there's a mistake on this bill. | **Saya rasa ada kesalahan pada bon ini.** *saya rasa ada cesalahan pada bon inee*

I've made ... telephone calls. | **Saya pakai telwpon ... kali.** *saya pakay telepon ... calee*

I've taken ... from the mini-bar. | **Saya ambil ... dari mini bar.** *saya ambil ... daree minee bar*

Can I have an itemized bill? | **Bisa saya dapatkan bon yang terperinci?** *bisa saya dapatkan bon yang terperincee*

Could I have a receipt, please? | **Bisa tolong saya minta tanda terima?** *bisa tolong saya minta tanda terrima*

Eating Out

Restaurants

In places such as Jakarta and Bali, large hotels offer the usual
international cuisine as well as a wide range of richly spiced
Indonesian-style dishes.

Warung

Warungs (street stalls) and **kaki lima** (food carts) are a familiar
part of the Indonesian scene. They are simple open-air eateries
providing a small range of dishes based on rice and one meat
or vegetable. You will find plenty congregated in the night
markets (**pasar malam**). You should be careful, however, not to
eat raw or undercooked food from these stalls and should
avoid them altogether if you have any doubts about hygiene.

Rumah makan

These eating houses are sometimes also known by the more
westernized term **restoran**. They may supply similar fare to the
warung but generally offer a wider choice of meat.

In most parts of Indonesia, you will find a **rumah makan Padang**
named after the Sumatran capital from where the style of cuisine
they offer originates. Customers are offered a wide selection of
hot and spicy dishes and only pay for what they eat.

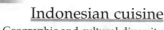

Indonesian cuisine

Geographic and cultural diversity, combined with a long history of foreign colonists and visiting merchants, have produced a unique cuisine.

The Chinese introduced **nasi goreng** (fried rice with vegetables) and **mie** (noodles), the Indians brought curries, and the Dutch sweets and cakes. More recently, western fast-food chains and Japanese and Thai restaurants have become a common feature in the cities.

Regional cuisine

Many dishes served in restaurants, both inside and outside Indonesia, originate in Java and Sumatra. Coastal areas traditionally use a wide range of spices and flavorings. Sumatran cooking is hot and spicy. Javanese cooking uses chili and other spices but the heat is mellowed by the use of sugar. The third region of Indonesia popular with tourists is Bali and Lombok. Here you will find the well-known **sate** (small pieces of meat roasted on a skewer); poultry is also popular. Roasted suckling pig (**babi guling**) is a traditional Balinese dish.

In Kalimantan you will not find a distinctive traditional cuisine as most of the townspeople come from other parts of Indonesia. That said, wild boar roasted over a fire is one specialty. Sulawesi has an extensive coastline and therefore offers a wide range of fish dishes.

Ramadan

Ramadan is one of the most important months of the Muslim calendar. During this time Muslims fast between the hours of sunrise and sunset.

During Ramadan many restaurants are closed in Muslim regions of the country. Those restaurants owned by non-Muslims will open, but may screen to obscure their operations in deference to those fasting. Ask around for those that are open.

A table for …, please.	**Tolong meja untuk … orang.** _tolong meja untuk … orang_
1/2/3/4	**satu/dua/tiga/empat** _satoo/dua/tiga/ermpat_
Thank you.	**Terima kasih.** _terrima casee_
The bill, please.	**Tolong bon.** _tolong bon_

Finding a place to eat Mencari tempat makan

Can you recommend a good restaurant?	**Bisa anda sarankan restoran yang enak?** _bisa anda sarancan restoran yang enak_
Is there a(n) … restaurant near here?	**Apa ada restoran … di dekat sini?** _apa ada restoran … dee decat sinee_
Chinese	**Cina** _china_
fish	**khusus ikan** _khusus ican_
inexpensive	**murah** _mura_
Italian restaurant	**restoran italia** _restoran italia_
Japanese	**Jepang** _jerpang_
traditional local restaurant	**restoran tradisional** _restoran tradisional_
vegetarian restaurant	**restoran makan sayur saja** _restoran macan sayur saja_
Where can I find a …?	**Dimana saya bisa temukan …?** _dimana saya bisa temucan_
burger stand	**penjual burger** _pernjual burger_
café	**kafe** _cafe_
ice cream parlor	**restoran es krim** _restoran es crim_
restaurant with a terrace/ garden	**restoran yang ada teras/halaman** _restoran yang ada terras/halaman_
fast-food restaurant	**restoran cepat siap** _restoran chepat siap_

DIRECTIONS ➤ 94

Reservations Memesan meja

I'd like to reserve a table …	**Saya mau pesan meja … orang.** *saya mow pesan meja … orang*
for two	**untuk dua** *untuk dua*
for this evening/ tomorrow at …	**untuk malam ini/besok jam …** *untuk malam inee/besok jam*
We'll come at 8:00.	**Kami akan datang jam delapan.** *camee acan datang jam derlapan*
A table for two, please.	**Tolong, meja untuk dua orang.** *tolong meja untuk dua orang*

Untuk jam berapa?	For what time?
Atas nama siapa?	What's the name, please?
Maaf. Kami penuh sekali.	I'm sorry. We're very busy/full.
Kami akan ada meja kosong … menit lagi.	We'll have a free table in … minutes.
Tolong kembali … menit lagi.	Please come back in … minutes.

Where to sit Tempat duduk

Could we sit …?	**Bisa kami duduk …?** *bisa camee duduk*
over there/outside	**di sana/di luar** *dee sana/di luar*
in a non-smoking area	**di tempat bebas rokok** *dee termpat bebas rocok*

– Saya mau memesan meja untuk malam ini.
(I'd like to reserve a table for this evening.)
– *Untuk berapa orang? (For how many people?)*
– Untuk empat orang. (For four.)
– *Untuk jam berapa? (For what time?)*
– Kami akan datang jam delapan.
(We'll come at 8:00.)
– *Atas nama siapa? (What's the name, please?)*
– Smith. (Smith.)
– *Baik. Terima kasih. (That's fine. Thank you.)*

Ordering Memesan

Waiter!/Waitress! *(to younger waiter/waitress)*	**Mas/Mbak!** *mas/mbak*
Waiter!/Waitress! *(to older waiter/waitress)*	**Pak/Bu!** *pak/boo*
Do you have a set menu?	**Apa ada menu paket?** *apa ada mernu pacet*
Can you recommend some typical local dishes?	**Bisa anda sarankan makanan khas daerah ini?** *bisa anda sarancan macanan khas daera inee*
Could you tell me what … is?	**Bisa anda terangkan apa … itu?** *bisa anda terangcan apa … itoo*
I'd like a bottle/glass of …	**Saya mau satu botol/satu gelas …** *saya mow satoo botol/satoo gerlas*

Apa anda sudah siap untuk memesan?	Are you ready to order?
Anda mau pesan apa?	What would you like?
Apa anda mau pesan minum dulu?	Would you like to order drinks first?
Saya menyarankan …	I recommend …
Kami belum dapat …	We haven't got …
Selamat makan.	Enjoy your meal.

– *Apa anda sudah siap untuk memesan?*
    (Are you ready to order?)

– *Bisa anda menyarankan makanan
        khas daerah ini?*
  (Can you recommend a typical local dish?)

– *Ya. Saya usul gudeg.*
    (Yes. I recommend the gudeg.)

– Baik, saya pesan yang itu.
    (OK, I'll have that, please.)

– *Baik. Dan anda mau minum apa?*
(Certainly. And what would you like to drink?)

– Tolong satu gelas teh. (A glass of tea, please.)

DRINKS ➤ 50; MENU READER ➤ 52

Side dishes Pesanan tambahan

Could I have ... without the ...?	**Bisa saya pesan ... tanpa ...?** *bisa saya pesan ... tanpa*
With a side order of ...	**Dengan pesanan tambahan ...** *dengan persanan tambahan*
Could I have salad instead of vegetables, please?	**Tolong sayur diganti dengan salad?** *tolong sayur digantee dengan salad*
Does the meal come with ...?	**Apa makanan sudah termasuk ...?** *apa macanan suda termasuk*
vegetables/potatoes	**sayur/kentang** *sayur/centang*
rice/pasta	**nasi/pasta** *nasee/pasta*
Do you have any ...?	**Ada ...?** *ada*
ketchup/mayonnaise	**saus tomat/mayones** *sows tomat/mayones*
I'd like ... with that.	**Saya mau ... dengan itu.** *saya mow ... dengan itoo*
vegetables/salad	**sayur/salad** *sayur/salad*
potatoes/fries [chips]	**kentang/kentang goreng** *centang/centang goreng*
sauce	**saus** *sows*
ice	**es** *es*
May I have some ...?	**Boleh saya minta ...?** *bole saya minta*
bread	**roti** *rotee*
butter	**mentega** *merntega*
lemon	**jeruk nipis** *jerruk nipis*
mustard	**mustar** *mustar*
pepper/salt	**merica/garam** *merricha/garam*
sugar	**gula** *gula*

General requests Permintaan umum

Could I/we have a(n)
(clean) …, please?
**Tolong saya minta …
(bersih)?** _tolong saya
minta … (bersi)_

ashtray **asbak** _asbak_

cup/glass **cangkir/gelas** _changcir/gerlas_

knife/fork/spoon **pisau/garpu/sendok/**
pisow/garpoo/sendok/

plate **piring** _piring_

napkin **serbet** _serbet_

I'd like some more …,
please.
Tolong, saya mau tambah …
tolong, saya mow tamba

That's all, thanks. **Itu saja. Terima kasih.**
itoo saja. terrima casi

Where are the restrooms
[toilets]?
Dimana kamar kecil?
dimana camar cechil

Special requirements Permintaan khusus

I can't eat food
containing …
**Saya tidak bisa makan makanan
yang mengandung …** _saya tidak
bisa macan macanan yang
mengandung_

salt/sugar **garam/gula** _garam/gula_

Do you have any dishes/
drinks for diabetics?
**Apa ada makanan/minuman untuk
penderita penyakit kencing manis?**
_apa ada macanan/minuman untuk
pernderita pernyacit cenching manis_

Do you have vegetarian
dishes?
Apa ada makanan sayur saja?
apa ada macanan sayur saja

For the children Untuk anak-anak

Do you have a children's
menu?
Apa ada menu untuk anak-anak?
apa ada mernoo untuk anak anak

Could you bring a child's
seat, please?
Tolong saya minta kursi anak-anak?
tolong saya minta cursee anak anak

CHILDREN ➤ 113

Fast food/Café
Makanan cepat siap/Kafe

Something to drink Minuman

I'd like (a) …	**Saya mau …** _saya mow_
tea/coffee	**teh/kopi** _te/copee_
black/with milk	**hitam/pakai susu** _hitam/pacay susoo_
lemonade/fruit juice	**limun/jus buah** _limun/jus bua_
I'd like a … of red/ white wine.	**Saya mau … anggur merah/putih.** _saya mow … anggur mera/puti_
glass/bottle	**gelas/botol** _gerlas/botol_
beer	**bir** _bir_

And to eat Makanan

A piece/slice of …, please.	**Tolong, satu/sepotong …** _tolong satoo/serpotong_
cake/pie	**cake/pie**
I'd like two of those.	**Saya minta yang itu dua.** _saya minta yang itoo dua_
burger/fries	**burger/kentang goreng** _burger/centang goreng_
omelet/pizza/sandwich	**telur dadar/pizza/sandwich** _terlur dadar/pizza/sandwich_
ice cream	**es krim** _es crim_
A … portion, please.	**Tolong, satu porsi …** _tolong satoo porsee_
small/regular [medium]/ large	**kecil/sedang/besar** _cerchil/serdang/bersar_
It's to go [take away].	**Untuk dibawa pulang.** _untuk dibawa pulang_
That's all, thanks.	**Itu saja, terima kasih.** _itoo saja terrima casi_

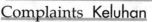

> – *Anda mau pesan apa?*
> (*What would you like to order?*)
> – Tolong kopi dua. (2 coffees, please.)
> – *Hitam atau pakai susu?* (*Black or with milk?*)
> – Tolong pakai susu. (With milk, please.)
> – *Mau pesan makan?* (*Anything to eat?*)
> – Itu saja, terima kasih. (That's all, thanks.)

Complaints Keluhan

I have no knife/fork/spoon.	**Saya tidak punya pisau/garpu/ sendok** _saya tidak punya pisow/ garpoo/sendok_
There must be some mistake.	**Pasti ada kesalahan.** _pastee ada cesalahan_
That's not what I ordered.	**Itu bukan yang saya pesan.** _itoo bucan yang saya pesan_
I asked for …	**Saya tadi pesan …** _saya tadee pesan_
I can't eat this.	**Saya tidak bisa makan ini.** _saya tidak bisa macan inee_
The meat is …	**Daging …** _daging_
overdone/underdone	**terlalu lembek/belum matang** _terlaloo lembek/berlum matang_
too tough	**terlalu keras** _terlaloo cerras_
This is too bitter/sour.	**Ini terlalu pahit/asam.** _inee terlaloo/pahit/asam_
The food is cold.	**Makanan dingin.** _macanan dingin_
This isn't fresh.	**Ini tidak segar.** _inee tidak sergar_
How much longer will our food be?	**Berapa lama lagi kami harus tunggu makanan kami?** _berrapa lama lagee camee harus tunggoo macanan camee_
I'd like to speak to the head waiter.	**Saya mau berbicara dengan kepala pelayan.** _saya mow berbichara dengan cepala perlayan_

41

Paying Bayar

I'd like to pay.	**Saya mau bayar.** _saya mow bayar_
The bill, please.	**Tolong bon.** _tolong bon_
We'd like to pay separately.	**Kami mau bayar sendiri-sendiri.** _camee mow bayar serndiree serndiree_
It's all together, please.	**Tolong dijadikan satu.** _tolong dijadican satoo_
I think there's a mistake in this bill.	**Saya rasa ada kesalahan pada bon ini.** _saya rasa ada cesalahan pada bon inee_
What is this amount for?	**Untuk apa jumlah yang ini?** _untuk apa jumla yang inee_
I didn't have that. I had …	**Saya tadi tidak makan itu. Saya makan …** _saya tadee tidak macan itoo. saya macan_
Is service included?	**Apa pelayanan sudah termasuk?** _apa perlayanan suda termasuk_
Can I pay with this credit card?	**Bisa saya bayar dengan kartu kredit?** _bisa saya bayar dengan cartoo credit_
Could I have a receipt, please?	**Tolong saya minta tanda terima?** _tolong saya minta tanda terrima_

– Mas! Tolong bon. (Waiter! The bill, please.)

– Baik. Ini dia. (Certainly. Here you are.)

– Apa pelayanan sudah termasuk?
(Is service included?)

– Ya, sudah termasuk. (Yes, it is.)

– Bisa saya bayar dengan kartu kredit?
(Can I pay with this credit card?)

– Ya, tentu saja. (Yes, of course.)

– Terima kasih. Makanan tadi enak sekali.
(Thank you. That was a very good meal.)

Course by course

Breakfast Makan pagi

I'd like …	**Saya mau …** _saya mow_
bread/butter	**roti/mentega** _rotee/merntega_
eggs	**telur** _terlur_
boiled/fried/scrambled	**rebus/mata sapi/dadar aduk** _rerbus/mata sapee/dadar aduk_
fruit juice	**jus buah** _jus bua_
honey	**madu** _madoo_
jam	**selai** _serlay_
milk	**susu** _susoo_
rolls	**roti kadet** _rotee cadet_
toast	**roti bakar** _rotee bacar_

Snacks Jajanan

asinan sayur/buah _asinan sayur/bua_
Salted vegetables/fruits: vegetables and fruits pickled in spiced salt water.

manisan _manisan_
Candied fruits or sweetmeats. These are served cold as a relish or side dish, or served hot and added to main courses dishes as a garnish.

lumpia _lumpia_
Spring rolls.

mpek-mpek _mpek mpek_
Fried pastry made of fish and flour.

martabak _martabak_
Thick pancake.

rujak _rujak_
Fruit salad with spicy palm sugar sauce.

jagung bakar _jagung bacar_
Roasted corn.

emping _emping_
Potato chips [crisps] made from **melinjo** nuts.

Soups Sop

sop ikan *sop ikan*
A favorite fish soup made of fish heads, starfruit, lemon grass, and chili.

sop buntut *sop buntut*
Oxtail soup is very fatty and oily and therefore should be served very hot. It is usually eaten with rice.

sop babat *sop babat*
Tripe soup, a favorite Indonesian dish.

soto ayam	*soto ayam*	chicken soup
sayur asam	*sayur asam*	sour vegetable soup
sayur lodeh	*sayur lode*	young jackfruit soup
sayur bayam	*sayur bayam*	spinach soup
sop kacang merah	*sop cachang mera*	red bean soup
sop jagung	*sop jagung*	corn soup

Egg dishes Masakan telur

telur asin *terlur asin*
Boiled eggs steeped in a salty water for a certain period (the longer the better), sometimes eaten by themselves (without rice). This is also a way of making boiled eggs last longer.

telur rebus	*terlur rerbus*	boiled eggs
telur dadar	*terlur dadar*	omelet
telur pindang	*terlur pindang*	spiced eggs in coconut sauce
telur dadar aduk	*terlur dadar aduk*	scrambled eggs

Fish and seafood
Makanan ikan dan makanan laut

cumi-cumi	*chumee chumee*	squid
bandeng	*bandeng*	milkfish
kepiting	*cerpiting*	crab
teri	*terree*	dried anchovies
udang barong	*oodang barong*	lobster
kerang	*cerrang*	clams
ikan bawal	*ican bawal*	pomfret
tiram	*tiram*	oysters
belut	*berlut*	eel
udang	*oodang*	shrimp [prawns]
ikan lele	*ican lele*	catfish
ikan hiu	*ican hiu*	shark
ikan tongkol	*ican tongcol*	tuna
ikan tenggiri	*ican tenggiree*	mackerel
ikan kakap	*ican cacap*	perch
ikan kerapu	*ican cerapoo*	grouper
ikan mas	*ican mas*	carp
ikan gurame	*ican gurame*	gurami

teri *terree*
Anchovies are salted and dried to make them last longer. A favorite dish is one of fried anchovies mixed with peanut and chili sauce.

kerang *cerrang*
Steamed clams are popular in Indonesia and are often served with a hot chili and pineapple sauce.

ikan lele *ican lele*
A common dish of catfish served fried with chili sauce and hot steamed rice.

Meat and poultry Daging dan ayam

daging babi asin	_daging babee asin_	bacon
daging sapi	_daging sapee_	beef
daging ayam	_daging ayam_	chicken
daging bebek	_daging bebek_	duck
daging babi	_daging babee_	pork
daging kelinci	_daging cerlinchee_	rabbit
sosis	_sosis_	sausages
bistik	_bistik_	steak
daging kalkun	_daging calcun_	turkey
daging sapi muda	_daging sapee muda_	veal

rendang _rendang_
This dish of meat cooked in spiced coconut milk and spices until the liquid evaporates can be found in almost all traditional Indonesian restaurants.

daging kambing _daging cambing_
This translates as 'goat meat'. There are basically three types of goat dishes: goat kebab (**sate kambing**), goat curry (**gule kambing**) and goat soup (**sop kambing**).

betawi _bertawee_
This traditional dish from Jakarta uses veal mixed with **emping** (melinjo), spring onions, tomato, and lime juice.

Meat cuts potongan daging

has dalam	_has dalam_	fillet steak
has luar	_has luar_	sirloin steak
daging pantat	_daging pantat_	rump steak
bistik T-bone	_bistik tee bon_	T-bone steak
hati	_hatee_	liver
babat	_babat_	tripe
potongan	_potongan_	chops
kaki	_cacee_	leg
sayatan	_sayatan_	cutlet, escalope

Vegetables Sayuran

kol	*col*	cabbage
wortel	*wortel*	carrots
tauge	*towge*	beansprouts
ketimun	*certimun*	cucumber
terung	*terrung*	eggplant [aubergine]
bawang putih	*bawang puti*	garlic
kacang buncis	*cachang bunchis*	french beans
kacang panjang	*cachang panjang*	runner beans
jamur	*jamur*	mushrooms
bawang bombay	*bawang bombay*	onions
paprika (merah/hijau)	*paprica (mera/hijow)*	peppers (red/green)
kentang	*centang*	potatoes
bawang merah	*bawang mera*	shallots
daun bawang	*down bawang*	spring onions
tomat	*tomat*	tomatoes
bayam	*bayam*	spinach

kangkung *cangcung*
This variety of spinach is the most common vegetable in Indonesia and is usually served stir-fried, mixed with chili and dried shrimp.

ubi *oobee*
Sweet potatoes are often served as a spicy potato chip [crisp].

sayur bayam *sayur bayam*
Spinach soup is very common in Indonesia. The soup is made from fresh spinach boiled with garlic and salt.

urap *oorap*
A vegetable dish with grated coconut and shrimp paste. It can be served as a main dish or as an accompaniment.

Salad salad

gado-gado _gado gado_

A dish of mixed vegetables with peanut sauce. Lightly steamed vegetables (cabbage, spinach, legumes) mixed with peanut sauce are served with **tempe** (cooked soybean paste), tofu and prawn crackers.

lalap _lalap_

Raw vegetables in a spicy sauce.

Acar _achar_

The word **acar** literally means 'pickle' or 'pickled.' Vinegar, sugar, and salt are used in the pickling process. There are many varieties of pickles, and they are usually served as side dishes.

Rice and noodles Nasi dan mie

In Indonesia rice (**nasi**) is an important part of many meals. Rice is served in an individual dish or is mixed with other food (**nasi campur**). The rice is short grained but is not as sticky as Japanese rice. Indonesians think that no main dish is complete without rice.

nasi campur	rice mixed with meat and vegetable side dishes
nasi uduk	rice cooked in coconut milk
nasi goreng istimewa	rice mixed with lamb curry
nasi kebuli	fried rice served with egg, chicken, lamb
ketupat	boiled rice wrapped in coconut leaves

Noodles dishes (**bakmie/mie**) are very popular. There are plenty of restaurants that only serve noodles.

bakmi bakso	noodles served with meatballs in soup
bakmi pangsit	noodles served with minced meat and prawn dumplings in soup
bakmi goreng	fried noodles mixed with meat and vegetables

Sauces Saus

saus tomat	*sows tomat*	tomato sauce
kecap	*cechap*	soy sauce
sambel	*sambal*	chili sauce

Dessert pencuci mulut

agar-agar	jello [jelly]
es krim	ice cream
rujak	fruit salad with spicy palm sugar sauce
es cendol	a drink made of rice flour with palm sugar and coconut milk
es campur	ice mixed with fruits and syrup

Fruit Buah

pisang	*pisang*	bananas
belimbing	*berlimbing*	starfruit
bangkuang	*bangcuang*	juicy tuber
anggur	*anggur*	grapes
nanas	*nanas*	pineapple
jeruk	*jerruk*	oranges
sirsak	*sirsak*	soursop
jambu	*jamboo*	guava
mangga	*mangga*	mango
kelapa	*cerlapa*	coconut
semangka	*sermangca*	watermelon
srikaya	*sricaya*	custard apple
sawo	*sawo*	sapodilla plum
semangka	*sermangca*	watermelon
klengkleng	*clengcleng*	longan
rambutan	*rambutan*	rambutan
nanas	*nanas*	pineapple
manggis	*manggis*	mangosteen
salak	*salak*	snakeskin fruit
duku	*ducu*	langsat
apokat	*apocat*	avocado
nangka	*nangca*	jackfruit

49

Drinks Minuman

Many of the Dutch-built breweries still supply beer.
The three popular brands are Bintang, San Miguel,
and Anker. Green Sands is a mild beer-lemonade
shandy. In some districts you will find **tuak** (palm wine).
Brem and **badik** are both rice wines. Chinese restaurants may
also serve **arak**, which is also made from rice.

Do you have … beer?	**Apa ada bir …?** _apa ada bir …_
bottled/draught [draft]	**botol/draft** _botol/draf_
beer	**bir** _bir_
stout	**bir hitam** _bir hitam_
Balinese rice wine	**brem** _brem_
palm wine	**tuak** _tuak_

Wine anggur

A little wine is produced in Java, but you will rarely come across
it. In international hotels you are more likely to find foreign
wines, which can be expensive.

Can you recommend a … wine?	**Bisa anda sarankan anggur … yang mana?** _bisa anda sarancan anggur … yang mana_
red/white/blush [rosé]	**merah/putih/ros** _mera/puti/ros_

Spirits and liqueurs Minuman keras

You will find most spirits and liqueurs are available in the
international hotels, usually known by their original names: gin,
whisky, vodka, etc.

straight/neat	**tanpa campuran/murnee** _tanpa champuran/murnee_
on the rocks [with ice]	**pakai es** _pacay es_
with water/tonic water	**pakai air/pakai air tonik** _pacay air/pacay air tonik_
I'd like a single/double …	**Saya mau single/double…** _saya mow single/double_

Non-alcoholic drinks
Minuman tidak beralkohol

Non-alcoholic beverages include a myriad of fresh fruit drinks, branded bottled drinks and mineral water. Cold, sweet bottled tea is an excellent drink in the heat.

Tea and coffee are both grown in Indonesia. Tea is practically the national beverage.

Be careful when drinking water – it should be well boiled. You may find it easiest outside your hotel (where the water should have been boiled) to drink fresh fruit juices without ice, or tea.

bandrek _bandrek_

This is a drink made of ginger and it is served hot. You can ask for a raw egg, milk or honey, or even a mixture of all three, to be added. The full version is known by the abbreviation **STMJ**: this stands for **susu** (milk), **telur** (egg), **madu** (honey), and **jahe** (ginger).

I'd like …	**Saya mau** _saya mow_
fresh coconut juice	**es kelapa muda** _es celapa muda_
fruit juice	**jus buah** _jus bua_
orange/pineapple/tomato	**jeruk/nanas/tomat** _jerruk/nanas/tomat_
hot chocolate	**coklat panas** _choclat_
mineral water	**air mineral** _air mineral_
carbonated/non-carbonated [still]	**air soda/acqua** _air soda/acwa_

Menu Reader

This Menu Reader gives listings under main food headings. You will see that the Indonesian words are shown in large type with the aim of helping you to identify, from a menu that has no English, at least the basic ingredients making up a dish.

Meat, and poultry

daging	_daging_	meat (general)
sapi	_sapee_	beef
kambing	_kambing_	goat
domba	_domba_	mutton
babi	_babee_	pork
ayam	_ayam_	chicken
bebek	_bebek_	duck
burung dara	_burungo dara_	pigeon
sosis	_sosis_	sausages
hati	_hatee_	liver

Fish and seafood

ikan	_ican_	fish (general)
kepiting	_kerpiting_	crab
udang barong	_oodang barong_	lobster
bandeng	_bandeng_	milkfish
kerang	_kerrang_	clams
gurita	_gurita_	octopus
udang	_oodang_	shrimp [prawn]
belut	_berlut_	eel
cumi-cumi	_chumee chumee_	squid
ikan tongkol	_ican tongcol_	tuna
ikan hiu	_ican hiu_	shark

Vegetables

sayur	*sayur*	vegetable(s) (general)
kacang buncis	*cachang bunchis*	green beans
bayam	*bayam*	spinach
kentang	*centang tomat*	pototoes
tomat	*tomat*	tomatoes
daun selada	*down serlada*	lettuce
ketimun	*certimun*	cucumber
kol	*col*	cabbage
wortel	*wortel*	carrots
bawang bombay	*bawang bombay*	onions
bawang putih	*bawang puti*	garlic
jagung	*jagung*	corn
daun salad	*down salad*	salad (general)

buah	_bua_	fruit (general)
apel	_apel_	apples
jeruk	_jerruk_	oranges
pisang	_pisang_	bananas
melon	_melon_	melons
per	_per_	pears
belimbing	_berlimbing_	starfruit
kelapa	_cerlapa_	coconut
korma	_corma_	dates
nanas	_nanas_	pineapple
alpokat	_alpocat_	avocado
mangga	_mangga_	mangos

Staples: bread, rice, pasta, etc.

roti	_rotee_	bread
nasi	_nasee_	rice (cooked)
bihun	_bihun_	rice noodles
spaghetti	spag_etee_	pasta
sagu	_sagu_	sago
kacang-kacangan	_cachang-cachangan_	beans
mi	mee	noodles

Basics

garam	_garam_	salt
merica	mer_icha_	pepper
cuka	_chuca_	vinegar
minyak zaitun	_minyak zaitun_	olive oil
minyak wijen	_minyak wijen_	sesame oil
asam	_asam_	tamarind

Herbs and spices

cabe	_chabe_	chili
daun sup	_down sup_	parsley
ketumbar	_kertumbar_	coriander
jahe	_jahe_	ginger
sereh	_sereh_	lemon grass
cengkeh	_chengce_	clove
segar	_sergar_	fresh
kering	_kerring_	dried
tepung	_terpung_	flour
jinten	_jinten_	cumin
pala	_pala_	nutmeg
kaya manis	_cayoo manis_	cinnamon

Basic cooking styles

panggang	_panggang_	grilled
goreng	_goreng_	fried
asap	_asap_	smoked
rebus	_rerbus_	boiled
rendam	_rendam_	marinated
bakar	_bacar_	baked
kukus	_cucus_	steamed
potongan segi empat	_potongan sergee ermpat_	diced
bumbu acar	_bumboo achar_	pickled
mentah	_menta_	raw
isi	_eesee_	stuffed

Classic dishes

ayam bakar	*ayam bacar*	charcoal grilled chicken
babi guling	*babee guling*	barbecued whole pig
bubur manado	*bubar manado*	rice porridge served with vegetable soup and fish
rendang	*rendang*	meat cooked in spiced coconut milk and spices until the liquid evaporates
gado-gado	*gado-gado*	vegetable salad with peanut sauce
gulai kambing	*gulay cambing*	mutton/goat meat cooked in spiced coconut milk
nasi goreng	*nasee goreng*	fried rice
ketoprak	*certoprak*	vegetables with rice noodles and tofu in peanut sauce
laksa ayam	*lacsa ayam*	rice noodle soup with chicken and coconut milk
sate ayam	*sate ayam*	chicken kebab
gudeg	*gudeg*	young jackfruit cooked in coconut milk with spices

Drinks

minuman	*minuman*	drinks (general)
air	*air*	water
susu	*susoo*	milk
teh	*te*	tea
kopi	*copee*	coffee
bir	*bir*	beer
anggur	*anggur*	wine
wiski	*wiscee*	whisky
gin	*jin*	gin

sari buah	_saree bua_	(fruit) juice
sari buah jeruk	_saree bua jerruk_	orange juice
sari buah melon	_saree bua melon_	melon juice
limun	_limun_	lemonade
cola	_cola_	Coke
air soda	_air soda_	soda water
air tonik	_air tonik_	tonic water
susu cocok	_susoo chochok_	milkshake
air mineral	_air mineral_	mineral water

Snacks

kentang goreng	_centang goreng_	fries [chips]
burger	_burger_	burger
biskuit	_biscit_	cookies [biscuits]
keik	ceik	cake
roti sandwich	_rotee sandwich_	sandwich
kerupuk	cerrupuk	potato chips [crisps]
kacang	_cachang_	peanuts
rujak	_rujak_	fruit salad with spicy palm sugar sauce
jagung bakar	_jagung bacar_	grilled corn
pisang goreng	_pisang goreng_	fried banana
martabak	_martabak_	thick pancakes
lemper	_lemper_	banana leaf stuffed with rice and meat

Dairy/soya products

keju	_ce_joo	cheese
yogurt	_yo_gurt	yogurt
krim	crim	cream
mentega	mern_tega_	butter
susu	_su_soo	milk
telur	ter_lur_	eggs
tempe	_tempe_	soybean cake
tahu	_ta_hoo	soybean curd
kecap	_ke_chap	sweet soya sauce
tauco	_tow_co	fermented soya beans

Desserts

es krim	*escrim*	ice cream
puding	*puding*	pudding
buah segar	*bua sergar*	fresh fruit
krim karamel	*crim caramel*	crème caramel
agar-agar	*agar-agar*	jello [jelly]
dodol	*dodol*	brown sugar and coconut cake
rujak	*rujak*	spicy fruit salad
serikaya	*serricaya*	almond and kenori nut cake
pisang goreng	*pisang goreng*	fried bananas
kue bugis	*kwe bugis*	coconut cake
onde-onde	*onde-onde*	rice cakes

Travel

ESSENTIAL

1/2/3 ticket(s) to …	**satu/dua/tiga tiket ke …** *satoo/dua/tiga ticet ce*
To …, please.	**Tolong ke …** *tolong ce*
one-way [single]	**satu kali jalan** *satoo calee jalan*
round-trip [return]	**pulang pergi** *pulang pergee*
How much …?	**Berapa harga …?** *berrapa harga*

Safety Keamanan

Would you accompany me to the bus stop?	**Mau anda temani saya ke setopan bis?** *mow anda temanee saya ce sertopan bis*
I don't want to … on my own.	**Saya tidak mau …sendirian.** *saya tidak mow … serndirian*
stay here	**tinggal di sini** *tinggal dee sinee*
walk home	**berjalan pulang** *berjalan pulang*
I don't feel safe here.	**Saya tidak merasa aman di sini.** *saya tidak merrasa aman dee sinee*

POLICE ➤ 159; EMERGENCY ➤ 224

Arrival Kedatangan

For citizens of many countries (including Australia, Canada, Ireland, the U.K., and the U.S.) a visa is not necessary for entry and a stay of up to six months.

However, check your passport expiration date; Indonesia requires a passport valid for six months following the date of arrival.

Passport control Pemeriksaan paspor

We have a joint passport.	**Kami punya satu paspor gabungan.** *camee punya satoo paspor gabungan*
The children are on this passport.	**Anak-anak di paspor ini.** *anak anak dee paspor inee*
I'm here on vacation [holiday]/business.	**Saya di sini untuk liburan/bisnis.** *saya dee sinee untuk liburan/bisnis*
I'm just passing through.	**Saya hanya lewat saja.** *saya hanya lewat saja*
I'm going to …	**Saya pergi ke …** *saya pergee ce*
I'm on my own.	**Saya sendirian.** *saya serndirian*
I'm with my family.	**Saya bersama keluarga saya.** *saya bersama celuarga saya*
I'm with a group.	**Saya bersama rombongan.** *saya bersama rombongan*

Customs Bea Cukai

I have only the normal allowances.	**Saya hanya dapat uang jalan biasa.** *saya hanya dapat uang jalan biasa*
It's a gift.	**Ini hadiah.** *inee hadia*
It's for my personal use	**Ini untuk keperluan pribadi.** *inee untuk ceperluan pribadee*
I would like to declare …	**Saya mau laporkan …** *saya mow laporkan*

I don't understand.	**Saya tidak mengerti.** _saya tidak mengertee_
Does anyone here speak English?	**Apa ada orang di sini yang berba hasa Inggris?** _apa ada orang dee sinee yang berbahasa inggris_

Do you have anything to declare?	**Apa ada sesuatu yang mau dilaporkan?**
You must pay duty on this.	**Anda harus bayar cukai untuk ini.**
Where did you buy this?	**Dimana anda membeli ini?**
Please open this bag.	**Tolong buka tas ini.**
Do you have any more luggage?	**Apa anda punya tas yang lain lagi?**

PEMERIKSAAN PASPOR	passport control
PENYEBERANGAN PERBATASAN	border crossing
BEA CUKAI	customs
TIDAK ADA YANG DILAPORKAN	nothing to declare
BARANG-BARANG YANG DILAPORKAN	goods to declare
BARANG BEBAS CUKAI	duty-free goods

Duty-free shopping Toko bebas cukai

What currency is this in?	**Apa mata uang yang berlaku disini?** _apa mata uang yang berlacoo disinee_
Can I pay in …	**Bisa saya bayar dengan …** _bisa saya bayar dengan_
dollars	_dolar_
pounds	**pound** _pownd_
rupiah	**rupiah** _rupiah_

Plane Pesawat terbang

Tickets and reservations Tiket dan pemesanan

When is the … flight to New York?	**Kapan penerbangan … ke New York?** _capan pernerbangan … ce New York_
first/next/last	**pertama/berikut/terakhir** _pertama/berricut/terrakhir_
I'd like two … tickets to New York.	**Saya mau dua tiket … ke New York.** _saya mow dua ticet … ce New York_
one-way [single]	**sekali jalan** _sercalee jalan_
round-trip [return]	**pulang pergi** _pulang pergee_
first class	**kelas utama** _celas ootama_
business class	**kelas bisnis** _celas bisnis_
economy class	**kelas ekonomi** _celas economee_
How much is a flight to …?	**Berapa harga tiket penerbangan ke …?** _berrapa harga ticet pernerbangan ce_
I'd like to … my reservation for flight number …	**Saya mau … pemesanan saya untuk penerbangan nomor …** _saya mow … permesanan saya untuk pernerbangan nomor_
cancel/change/confirm	**batalkan/ubah/pastikan** _batalcan/ooba/pastican_

Inquiries about the flight
Keterangan tentang penerbangan

How long is the flight?	**Berapa lama penerbangan?** _berrapa lama pernerbangan_
What time does the plane leave?	**Jam berapa pesawat berangkat?** _jam berrapa persawat berrangcat_
What time will we arrive?	**Jam berapa kita akan tiba?** _jam berrapa cita acan tiba_

Checking in Checking in

Where is the check-in counter for flight …?	**Dimana meja check-in untuk penerbangan …?** *dimana meja check in untuk pernerbangan*
I have …	**Saya punya …** *saya punya*
three suitcases to check in	**tiga koper untuk check-in** *tiga coper untuk check in*
two carry-ons [pieces of hand luggage]	**dua tas tangan** *dua tas tangan*

Olong tiket/paspor anda.	Your ticket/passport, please.
Apa anda mau kursi dekat jendela atau dekat gang?	Would you like a window or an aisle seat?
Merokok atau tidak merokok?	Smoking or non-smoking?
Silahkan menuju ruang keberangkatan.	Please go through to the departure lounge.
Berapa banyak bagasi yang anda punya?	How many pieces of baggage do you have?
Bagasi anda berlebih.	You have excess baggage.
Anda harus bayar tambahan … rupiah.	You'll have to pay a supplement of … rupiah.
Itu terlalu berat/besar untuk tas tangan.	That's too heavy/large for a carry-on.
Apa anda sendiri yang mengepak tas ini?	Did you pack these bags yourself?
Apa ada barang tajam atau elektronik?	Do they contain any sharp or electronic items?

KEDATANGAN	arrivals
KEBERANGKATAN	departures
PEMERIKSAAN KEAMANAN	security check
JANGAN TINGGALKAN BARANG	do not leave bags unattended

BAGGAGE ➤ 71

Information Informasi

Is there any delay on flight …?	**Apa ada penundaan pada penerbangan …?** *apa ada penundaan pada pernerbangan*
How late will it be?	**Akan berapa lama keterlambat?** *acan berrapa lama ceterlambat*
Has the flight from … landed?	**Apa penerbangan dari … sudah mendarat?** *apa penerbangan daree … suda mendarat*
Which gate does flight … leave from?	**Dari gerbang yang mana penerbangan …berangkat?** *daree gerbang yang mana pernerbangan … berrangcat*

In-flight Dalam penerbangan

Could I have a drink/ something to eat, please?	**Tolong, bisa saya mendapat minuman/ sesuatu untuk dimakan?** *tolong bisa saya dapat minuman/sersuatoo untuk dimacan*
Please wake me for the meal.	**Tolong bangunkan saya waktu makan.** *tolong banguncan saya wactoo macan*
What time will we arrive?	**Jam berapa kita akan tiba?** *jam berrapa cita acan tiba*
An airsickness bag, please.	**Tolong, kantung muntah.** *tolong cantung muntah*

Arrival Kedatangan

Where is/are the …?	**Dimana …?** *dimana*
buses/car rental	**bis/sewa mobil** *bis/sewa mobil*
currency exchange	**penukaran uang** *pernucaran uang*
exit/taxis	**pintu keluar/taksi** *pintoo celuar/ taksee*
Is there a bus into town?	**Apa ada bis yang ke kota?** *apa ada bis yang ce cota*
How do I get to the … hotel?	**Bagaimana cara saya ke hotel …?** *bagaimana chara saya ce hotel*

BAGGAGE ➤ 71; CUSTOMS ➤ 67

Baggage bagasi

Porter! Excuse me! **Permisi, portir!**
permisee portir

Could you take my **Bisa anda bawa koper**
luggage to …? **saya ke …?** *bisa anda*
bawa coper saya ce

a taxi/bus **taksi/bis** *taksi/bis*

Where is/are (the) …? **Dimana …?** *dimana*

luggage carts [trolleys] **kereta dorong** *cereta dorong*

baggage check **pemeriksaan bagasi**
[left-luggage office] *permerricsa'an bagasee*

baggage claim **pengambilan bagasi**
perngambilan bagasee

Where is the luggage **Dimana koper dari penerbangan …?**
from flight …? *dimana coper daree pernerbangan*

Loss, damage, and theft
Kehilangan, Kerusakan, dan Pencurian

I've lost my baggage. **Saya kehilangan bagasi saya.**
saya cehilangan bagasee saya

My baggage has been **Bagasi saya dicuri.**
stolen. *bagasee saya dichuree*

My suitcase was damaged. **Koper saya rusak.**
koper saya rusak

What does your baggage look like?	**Seperti apa bentuk bagasi anda?**
Do you have the claim check [reclaim tag]?	**Apa anda punya tanda pengambilan?**
Your luggage …	**Koper anda …**
may have been sent to …	**mungkin terbawa ke …**
may arrive later today	**mungkin akan tiba nanti.**
Please come back tomorrow.	**Tolong datang kembali besok.**
Call this number to check if your baggage has arrived.	**Telepon nomor ini untuk mengetahui apa bagasi anda telah tiba.**

POLICE ➤ 159; COLOR ➤ 143

Traveling around Indonesia

Air

Indonesia has a fairly extensive network of flights provided by a variety of domestic airlines. Recently, domestic air travel has been in a state of flux. Air fares have risen sharply. However, for those with hard currency, air travel is still very cheap by world standards.

Each airline publishes a nationwide timetable. Try to get hold of one if you can. Overbooking is a problem so remember that it is essential to reconfirm your flight. Airlines accept credit cards, but don't expect to be able to use them in small offices on the outer islands.

Train

Train travel in Indonesia is restricted solely to Java and Sumatra. There are no railways on any of the other isalnds. There is a good train service running from one end of Java to the other. In the east it connects with the ferry service to Bali, and in the west with the ferry to Sumatra. In Java, trains are one of the easiest ways of getting around, and the most comfortable too. In Sumatra there is a limited train service.

Boat

Regular ferries connect all the islands. Ferries run daily or several times a week. Almost all ferries can carry larger vehicles; all will take motorbikes.

Pelni is the largest shipping line, servicing almost everywhere. It has modern air-conditioned ships that operate set routes around the islands on a two-weekly or monthly schedule.

MASUK	entrance
KELUAR	exit
INFORMASI	information
PEMESANAN TIKET	ticket reservations
KEDATANGAN	arrivals
KEBERANGKATAN	departures

Train Kereta api

To the station Ke stasiun

How do I get to the train station?	**Bagaimana cara saya ke stasiun?** *bagaimana chara saya ce stasiun*
Do trains to Bandung leave from … station?	**Apa kereta ke Bandung berangkat dari stasiun …?** *apa cereta ce bandung berrangcat daree stasiun*
How far is it?	**Berapa jauh?** *berrapa jow*
Can I leave my car there?	**Bisa saya tinggalkan mobil saya di sana?** *bisa saya tinggalcan mobil saya dee sana*

At the station Di stasiun

Where is/are the …?	**Dimana …?** *dimana*
baggage check [left-luggage office]	**pemeriksaan bagasi** *permerricsa'an bagasee*
currency exchange	**penukaran uang** *pernucaran uang*
information desk	**meja informasi** *meja informasee*
lost and found [lost property office]	**pengaduan barang hilang** *perngaduan barang hilang*
platforms	**peron** *perron*
snack bar	**warung makanan kecil** *warung macanan cechil*
ticket office	**penjualan tiket** *pernjualan ticet*
waiting room	**ruang tunggu** *ruang tunggoo*

DIRECTIONS ➤ 94

Tickets Tiket

I'd like a … ticket to Bandung.	**Saya mau tiket … ke Bandung.** _saya mow ticet ce bandung_
one-way [single]	**sekali jalan** _sercalee jalan_
round-trip [return]	**pulang pergi** _pulang pergee_
first/second class	**kelas utama/kelas dua** _celas ootama/celas dua_
discount [concessionary]	**potongan harga** _potongan harga_
I'd like to reserve a(n) … seat.	**Saya mau pesan … kursi.** _saya mow pesan … cursee_
aisle seat	**kursi dekat gang** _cursee decat gang_
window seat	**kursi dekat jendela** _cursee decat jerndela_
Is there a sleeping car [sleeper]?	**Apa ada gerbong untuk tidur?** _apa ada gerbong untuk tidur_
I'd like a(n) … berth.	**Saya mau tempat tidur …** _saya mow tempat tidur_
upper/lower	**di atas/di bawah** _dee atas/dee bawa_

Price Harga

How much is that?	**Berapa harga?** _berrapa harga_
Is there a discount for …?	**Apa ada potongan untuk …?** _apa ada potongan untuk_
children/families	**anak-anak/keluarga** _anak anak/celuarga_
senior citizens	**orang tua** _orang tua_
students	**pelajar** _perlajar_

Queries Pertanyaan

Could I have a timetable, please?

Tolong, bisa saya dapat jadwal? *tolong bisa saya dapat jadwal*

Is it a direct train?

Apa ini kereta langsung? *apa inee cereta langsung*

You have to change at …

Anda harus ganti di … *anda harus gantee dee*

How long is this ticket valid for?

Berapa lama tiket ini berlaku? *berrapa lama ticet inee berlacoo*

Can I return on the same ticket?

Bisa saya kembali dengan pakai tiket yang sama? *bisa saya cem balee dengan pakay ticet yang sama*

In which car [coach] is my seat?

Di gerbong yang mana kursi saya? *di gerbong yang mana cursee saya*

Is there a dining car on the train?

Apa ada gerbong makan di kereta api? *apa ada gerbong macan dee cerreta apee*

When is the … train to Bandung?

Kapan kereta api … ke Bandung? *capan cerreta apee … ce bandung*

first/next/last

pertama/berikut/yang terakhir *pertama/berricut/yang terrakhir*

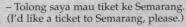

– Tolong saya mau tiket ke Semarang.
(I'd like a ticket to Semarang, please.)

– *Sekali jalan atau pulang pergi?*
(One way or round trip?)

– Tolong yang pulang pergi.
(Round trip, please.)

– *Semuanya tiga puluh ribu rupiah.*
(That's thirty thousand rupiah.)

– Apa saya harus ganti kereta api?
(Do I have to change trains?)

– *Ya, anda harus ganti di Cirebon.*
(Yes, you have to change at Cirebon.)

– Terima kasih. Sampai jumpa.
(Thank you. Good-bye.)

Train times Jam kereta api

How frequent are the trains to …?	**Berapa sering kereta api ke …?** *berrapa serring cerreta apee ce*
once/twice a day	**satu kali/dua kali sehari** *satoo/dua calee serharee*
five times a day	**lima kali sehari** *lima calee serharee*
every hour	**setiap jam** *setiap jam*
What time do they leave?	**Jam berapa mereka berangkat?** *jam berrapa merreca berrangcat*
on the hour	**setiap jam** *setiap jam*
20 minutes past the hour	**setiap jam lewat duapuluh menit** *setiap jam lewat duapulu mernit*
What time does the train stop at …?	**Jam berapa kereta api berhenti di …?** *jam berrapa cerreta apee berhentee dee*
What time does the train arrive in …?	**Jam berapa kereta api tiba di …?** *jam berrapa cerreta apee tiba dee*
How long is the trip [journey]?	**Berapa lama perjalanan?** *berrapa lama perjalanan*
Is the train on time?	**Apa kereta api tepat waktu?** *apa cerreta apee terpat wactoo*

Departures Keberangkatan

Which platform does the train to … leave from?	**Dari peron yang mana kereta api ke … berangkat?** *daree perron yang mana cerreta apee ce … berrangcat*
Where is platform 4?	**Dimana peron 4?** *dimana perron empatpulu tuju*
over there/on the left/right	**di sana/di sebelah kiri/kanan** *dee sana/dee serbela ciree/canan*
Where do I change for …?	**Dimana saya ganti kereta untuk …?** *dimana saya gantee cereta untuk*
How long will I have to wait for a connection?	**Berapa lama saya harus tunggu untuk kereta lanjutan?** *berrapa lama saya harus tunggu untuk cereta lanjutan*

Boarding Naik ke kereta

Is this the right platform for …?	**Apa ini peron untuk …?** *apa inee perron untuk*
Is this the train to …?	**Apa kereta api ini ke …?** *apa cerreta apee inee ce*
Is this seat taken?	**Apa kursi ini ada yang punya?** *apa cursee inee ada yang punya*
That's my seat.	**Itu kursi saya.** *itoo cursee saya*
Here's my reservation.	**Ini bukti pemesanan saya.** *inee buctee permesanan saya*
Are there any seats/ berths available?	**Apa masih ada kursi/tempat tidur yang tersedia?** *apa masi ada cursee/ tempat tidur yang tersedia*
Do you mind if …?	**Apa anda keberatan kalau …?** *apa anda ceberatan calow*
I sit here	**saya duduk di sini** *saya duduk dee sinee*
I open the window	**saya buka jendela** *saya buca jerndela*

During the trip Dalam perjalanan

How long are we stopping here for?	**Berapa lama kita akan berhenti di sini?** *berrapa lama cita acan berhentee dee sinee*
When do we get to …?	**Kapan kita akan sampai di …?** *capan cita acan sampay dee*
Where is the dining/ sleeping car?	**Dimana gerbong makan/tidur?** *dimana gerbong macan/tidur*
Where is my berth?	**Dimana tempat tidur saya?** *dimana tempat tidur saya*
I've lost my ticket.	**Saya kehilangan tiket** *saya cehilangan ticet*

REM BAHAYA	emergency brake
TANDA BAHAYA	alarm
PINTU OTOMATIS	automatic doors

Long-distance bus [Coach]
Bis jarak jauh

Where is the bus [coach] station?	**Dimana stasiun bis?** *dimana stasiun bis*
When's the next bus [coach] to …?	**Kapan bis ke … yang berikut?** *capan bis ce … yang berricut*
Where does it leave from?	**Darimana bis itu akan berangkat?** *darimana bis itoo acan berrangkat*
Where are the bus stops [coach bays]?	**Dimana setopan bis?** *dimana sertopan bis*
Does the bus [coach] stop at …?	**Apa bis berhenti di …?** *apa bis berhentee dee*
How long does the trip take?	**Berapa lama perjalanan ini?** *berrapa lama perjalanan inee*
Are there … on board?	**Apa ada … di dalam?** *apa ada … dee dalam*
refreshments/toilets	**minuman/kamar kecil** *minuman/camar cechil*

Bus Bis

Where is the bus station?	**Dimana terminal bis?** *dimana terminal bis*
Where can I get a bus to …?	**Darimana ada bis yang ke …?** *darimana ada bis yang ce …*
What time is the … bus to Surabaya?	**Jam berapa bis … ke Surabaya?** *jam berrapa bis … ce surabaya*

Anda harus ke setopan yang di sebelah sana	You need that stop over there.
Anda perlu naik bis nomor …	You need bus number …
Anda harus berganti bis di …	You must change buses at …

bus stop	**SETOPAN BIS**
no smoking	**DILARANG MEROKOK**
exit/emergency exit	**PINTU KELUAR/PINTU DARURAT**

DIRECTIONS ➤ 94; TIME ➤ 220

Buying tickets Pembelian tiket

Where can I buy tickets?

Dimana saya bisa membeli tiket? *dimana saya bisa belee ticet*

A ... ticket to Surabaya, please.

Tolong satu tiket ... ke Surabaya. *tolong satoo ticet ... ce surabaya*

one-way [single]

sekali jalan *sercalee jalan*

round-trip [return]

pulang pergi *pulang pergee*

How much is the fare to ...?

Berapa ongkos perjalanan ke ...? *berrapa ongcos perjalanan ce*

Traveling Perjalanan

Is this the right bus to ...?

Apa ini bis yang ke ...? *apa inee bis yang ce*

Could you tell me when to get off?

Bisa anda memberi tahu kapan saya turun? *bisa anda memberee tahoo capan saya turun*

Do I have to change buses?

Apa saya perlu ganti bis? *apa saya perloo gantee bis*

How many stops are there to ...?

Ada berapa setopan untuk ke ...? *ada berrapa sertopan untuk ce*

Next stop, please!

Tolong berhenti di setopan berikut! *tolong berhentee dee sertopan berricut*

– Permisi. Apa ini bis yang ke balai kota?
(Excuse me. Is this the right bus to
the town hall?)
– *Ya, nomor delapan. (Yes, number 8.)*
– Tolong satu ke balai kota.
(One to the town hall, please.)
– *Delapan ratus rupiah.*
(That's 800 rupiah.)
– Kapan saya harus turun?
(Could you tell me when to get off?)
– *Empat setopan dari sini. (It's four stops from here.)*

NUMBERS ➤ 216; DIRECTIONS ➤ 94

Rickshaws Becak

A **becak** is the Indonesian term for a rickshaw. Becaks can carry one or two people over relatively short distances through side roads. They are allowed on main roads only at certain times. There is no fixed charge – the amount being negotiated between the passenger(s) and driver at the outset. Ask around on the price range beforehand. Becak drivers can be asked to wait and to take you on to another place. There is, of course, an extra charge for this service based on agreement. They can also be hired on an hourly basis.

Where's the nearest rickshaw station?	**Dimana pangkalan becak yang terdekat?** *dimana pangcalan becha yang terdecat*
Can you take me/us to jalan Sabang?	**Bisa tolong ke jalan Sabang.** *bisa tolong ce jalan sabang*
How much is it to jalan Tosari?	**Berapa ke jalan Tosari?** *berrapa ce jalan tosaree*
Please drive slowly.	**Tolong jalan pelan pelan.** *tolong jalan pelan pelan*
That too expensive.	**Terlalu mahal.** *terlaloo mahal*
Can you go down a little?	**Bisa lebih murah?** *bisa lebi mura*
How long is the trip going to take?	**Berapa lama sampai ke tujuan?** *berrapa lama sampay ce tujuan*
No, that's my last offer.	**Tidak bisa kurang lagi.** *tidak bisa curang lagee*
Where are we?	**Dimana kita sekarang?** *dimana cita sercarang*
Please wait for me/us here.	**Tolong, tunggu saya/kami disini.** *tolong tunggoo saya/camee disinee*
How much is the extra charge for waiting?	**Berapa saya harus tambah untuk tunggu?** *berrappa saya harus tambah untuk tunggu*
How much is the cost per hour?	**Berapa sewa per jam?** *berrapa sewa per jam*

NUMBERS ➤ 216; BUYING TICKETS ➤ 74, 79

Ferry Feri

When is the … ferry to Gilimanuk?	**Kapan feri … ke Gilimanuk?** _capan feri … ce gilimanuk_
first/next/last	**pertama/berikut/yang terakhir** _pertama/berricut/yang terrakhir_
hovercraft/ship	**hovercraft/kapal** _hovercraf/capal_
A round-trip [return] ticket for …	**Satu tiket pulang pergi ke …** _satoo tiket pulang pergee ce_
one car and one trailer [caravan]	**satu mobil dan satu gandengan** _satoo mobil dan satoo gandengan_
two adults and three children	**dua dewasa dan tiga anak-anak** _dua dewasa dan tiga anak anak_
I want to reserve a … cabin.	**Saya ingin pesan kabin dengan …** _saya ingin pesan cabin dengan_
single/double	**satu tempat tidur/dua tempat tidur** _satoo tempat tidur/dua tempat tidur_

PELAMPUNG	life preserver [life belt]
SEKOCI PENOLONG	lifeboat
TEMPAT PENDAFTARAN	muster station
DILARANG MASUK	no access

Boat trips Pesiar dengan kapal

Is there a …?	**Apa ada …?** _apa ada_
boat trip/river cruise	**pesiar dengan kapal/pesiar melewati sungai** _pesiar dengan capal/pesiar melewati sungay_
What time does it leave?	**Jam berapa berangkat?** _jam berrapa berrangcat_
What time does it return?	**Jam berapa kembali?** _jam berrapa cembalee_
Where can we buy tickets?	**Dimana kami bisa beli tiket?** _dimana camee bisa belee tiket_

TIME ➤ 220; BUYING TICKETS ➤ 74, 79

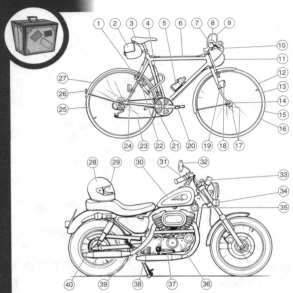

1 brake pad **kanvas rem**	21 lock **kunci**
2 bicycle bag **tas sepeda**	22 generator [dynamo] **dinamo**
3 seat **sadel**	23 chain **rantai**
4 pump **pompa**	24 rear light **lampu belakang**
5 water bottle **botol air**	25 rim **pelek**
6 frame **rangka**	26 reflectors **pemantul cahaya**
7 handlebars **setang**	27 fender [mudguard] **sayap roda**
8 bell **bel**	28 helmet **helem**
9 brake cable **kabel rem**	29 visor **kaca pelindung sinar matahari**
10 gear shift [lever] **pemindah gigi**	30 fuel tank **tangki bensin**
11 gear control cable	31 clutch **pedal kopling**
kabel pengendali gigi	32 mirror **cermin**
12 inner tube **ban dalam**	33 ignition switch **tombol starter**
13 front/back wheel	34 turn signal [indicator] **meteran**
roda depan/belakang	35 horn **klakson**
14 axle **as roda**	36 engine **mesin**
15 tire [tyre] **ban**	37 gear shift [lever] **pemindah persneling**
16 wheel **roda**	38 kick stand **pijakan kaki**
17 spokes **jari-jari**	39 exhaust pipe **knalpot**
18 bulb **bola lampu**	40 chain guard **rantai pengaman**
19 headlamp **lampu depan**	
20 pedal **pedal**	

REPAIRS ➤ *89*

Bicycle/Motorbike
Sepeda/Sepeda Motor

I'd like to rent a … **Saya mau sewa …**
saya mow sewa

3-/10-speed bicycle **sepeda dengan tiga/sepuluh gigi**
serpeda dengan tiga/serpuluh gigee

moped **moped** *moped*

motorbike **sepeda motor** *serpeda motor*

How much does it cost **Berapa sewa per hari/minggu?**
per day/week? *berrapa sewa per haree/minggoo*

Do you require a deposit? **Apa harus pakai uang muka?**
apa harus pakay uang muca

The brakes don't work. **Rem tidak jalan.** *rem tidak jalan*

There aren't any lights. **Tidak ada lampu.**
tidak ada lampoo

The front/rear tire [tyre] **Ban depan/belakang kempes.**
has a flat [puncture]. *ban depan/belacang cempes*

Hitchhiking Menumpang

Where are you heading? **Anda mau kemana?**
anda mow cemana

I'm heading for … **Saya mau ke …** *saya mow ce*

Is that on the way to …? **Apa itu dalam perjalanan ke …?**
apa itoo dalam perjalanan ce

Could you drop me off …? **Bisa anda turunkan saya …?**
bisa anda turuncan saya

here/at … **di sini/di …** *dee sinee/dee*

at the … exit **di jalan keluar ke …**
dee jalan cerluar ce

downtown **pusat kota** *pusat cota*

Thanks for giving me a lift. **Terima kasih atas tumpangan
jemputan.** *terrima casi atas
tumpangan jermputan*

DIRECTIONS ➤ 94; *NUMBERS* ➤ 216

Taxi/Cab Taksi

Where can I get a taxi?	**Dimana saya bisa dapatkan taksi?** *dimana saya bisa dapatkan tacsee*
Do you have the number for a taxi?	**Apa anda punya nomor telepon taksi?** *apa anda punya nomor telepon tacsee*
I'd like a taxi …	**Saya mau taksi …** *saya mow tacsee*
now	**sekarang** *sercarang*
in an hour	**dalam waktu satu jam** *dalam wactoo satoo jam*
The address is …	**Alamat adalah …** *alamat adala*
I'm going to …	**Saya mau pergi ke …** *saya mow pergee ce*
Please take me to (the) …	**Tolong antar saya ke …** *tolong antar saya ce*
airport	**lapangan terbang** *lapangan terbang*
train station	**stasiun kereta api** *stasiun cerreta apee*
this address	**alamat ini** *alamat inee*
How much is that?	**Berapa harga?** *berrapa harga*
Keep the change.	**Simpan saja kembalian.** *simpan saja cembalian*

> – Tolong antar saya ke stasiun kereta api.
> (Please take me to the train station.)
> – *Baik.* (Certainly.)
> – Berapa harga? (How much will it cost?)
> – *Tiga puluh ribu rupiah. … Nah sudah sampai.*
> (Thirty thousand rupiah. … Here we are.)
> – Terimakasih. Simpan saja kembalian.
> (Thank you. Keep the change.)

NUMBERS ➤ 216; DIRECTIONS ➤ 94

Car/Automobile Mobil

Indonesians drive on the left. Opportunities for self-drive are fairly limited, except in Bali and Lombok. Driving can be a stressful exercise – the roads are shared by pedestrians, animals, and food carts, and other drivers only add to the problems. If you have an accident, you may find yourself in trouble – as a foreigner you will almost certainly be blamed. It is more common and often cheaper to rent a car or minibus with a driver.

The price of car rental varies according to both location and vehicle. The major car rental companies have offices in the main cities.

For car or minibus rental with a driver included (but usually excluding gas, other than for city sightseeing) it is wise to bargain. If you want to find a driver for trips of a few days (or even weeks) negotiate a deal that covers both food and accommodations. It is generally wise to test out the driver for a day before heading off on a lengthy trip.

The price of gas is reasonably low in Indonesia. There are gas stations in larger towns, but out in the villages they can be difficult to find. Small roadside shops sell gas in small amounts. Look for signs that read **press ban**, or for crates of bottles with a **bensin** sign. Beware the gas from these stands which may be of dubious quality. Flat tires are usually repaired at small roadside stands called **tambal ban**.

Conversion Chart

km	1	10	20	30	40	50	60	70	80	90	100	110	120	130
miles	0.62	6	12	19	25	31	37	44	50	56	62	68	74	81

Car rental Sewa mobil

Where can I rent a car?	**Dimana saya bisa sewa mobil?** _dimana saya bisa sewa mobil_
I'd like to rent a(n) …	**Saya mau sewa …** _saya mow sewa_
2-/4-door car	**mobil dua/empat pintu** _mobil dua/empat pintoo_
automatic	**otomatis** _otomatis_
car with 4-wheel drive	**mobil four-wheel drive** _mobil four wheel drive_
car with air conditioning	**mobil dengan AC** _mobil dengan ase_
I'd like it for a day/week.	**Saya mau untuk satu hari/minggu.** _saya mow untuk satoo haree/ minggoo_
How much does it cost per day/week?	**Berapa harga per hari/minggu?** _berrapa harga per haree/minggoo_
Is insurance included?	**Apa sudah termasuk asuransi?** _apa suda termasuk asuransee_
Are there special weekend rates?	**Apa ada tarif khusus akhir pekan?** _apa ada tarif khusus akhir pekan_
Can I return the car at …?	**Bisa saya kembalikan mobil di …?** _bisa saya cembalican mobil dee_
What kind of fuel does it take?	**Apa jenis bahan bakar?** _apa jenis bahan bacar_
Where is the high [full]/ low [dipped] beam?	**Dimana tombol untuk lampu jauh/ dekat?** _dimana tombol untuk lampoo jow/decat_
Could I have full insurance?	**Bisa saya dapatkan asuransi penuh?** _bisa saya dapatcan asuransee penu_

Gas [Petrol] station Pompa bensin

Where's the next gas [petrol] station, please?
Dimana pompa bensin terdekat? _dimana pompa bensin terdecat_

Fill it up, please.
Tolong diisi penuh. _tolong diisee penu_

… liters, please.
Tolong … liter. _tolong … liter_

premium/regular
premium/biasa _premium/biasa_

diesel
solar _solar_

I'm at pump number …
Saya di pompa nomor … _saya di pompa nomor_

Where is the air pump/water?
Dimana pompa angin/air? _dimana pompa angin/air_

HARGA PER LITER   price per liter

Parking Parkir

Is there a parking lot [car park] nearby?
Apa ada tempat parkir di sekitar sini? _apa ada tempat parcir dee secitar sinee_

What's the charge per hour/day?
Berapa tarif per jam/hari? _berrapa tarif per jam/haree_

My car has been booted [clamped]. Who do I call?
Mobil saya diderek. Kemana harus saya mencari? _mobil saya diderek. cemana harus saya mencharee_

NUMBERS ➤ 216; DIRECTIONS ➤ 94

Breakdown Kerusakan

Where is the nearest garage?	**Dimana bengkel terdekat?**
	dimana bengcel terdecat
My car broke down.	**Mobil saya rusak**
	mobil saya rusak
Can you send a mechanic/tow [breakdown] truck?	**Bisa anda kirimkan tukang/ mobil penderek?**
	bisa anda cirimcan tucang/ mobil penderek
My license plate [registration] number is …	**Nomor pelat saya …**
	nomor perlat saya
The car is …	**Mobil …** *mobil*
on the highway [motorway]	**di jalan tol**
	dee jalan tol
2 km from …	**2 kilometer dari …**
	dua cilometer daree
How long will you be?	**Berapa lama anda akan sampai?**
	berrapa lama anda acan sampay

What's wrong? Apa masalah?

My car won't start.	**Mobil saya tidak bisa nyala.**
	mobil saya tidak bisa nyala
The battery is dead.	**Aki habis.**
	acee habis
I've run out of gas [petrol].	**Saya kehabisan bensin.**
	saya cehabisan bensin
I have a flat [puncture].	**Ban saya kempes.**
	ban saya cempes
There is something wrong with …	**Ada masalah dengan …**
	ada masala dengan
I've locked the keys in the car.	**Kunci saya tertinggal dalam mobil.**
	cunchee saya tertinggal dalam mobil

Repairs Perbaikan

Do you do repairs?

Apa anda bisa perbaiki kerusakan? *apa anda bisa perbaikee cerusacan*

Can you repair it?

Bisa anda perbaiki ini? *bisa anda perbaikee inee*

Please make only essential repairs.

Tolong perbaiki yang penting saja. *tolong perbaikee yang penting saja*

Can I wait for it?

Bisa saya tunggu? *bisa saya tunggoo*

Can you repair it today?

Bisa anda perbaiki hari ini? *bisa anda perbaikee haree inee*

When will it be ready?

Kapan ini selesai? *capan inee serlersay*

How much will it cost?

Berapa harga? *berrapa harga*

That's outrageous!

Itu keterlaluan! *itoo ceterlaluan*

Can I have a receipt for my insurance?

Bisa saya mendapatkan tanda terima untuk asuransi saya? *bisa saya dapatcan tanda terrima untuk asuransee saya*

... tidak bekerja.	The ... isn't working.
Saya tidak punya suku cadang yang diperlukan.	I don't have the necessary parts.
Saya harus memesan suku cadang.	I will have to order the parts.
Saya hanya bisa memperbaiki untuk sementara saja.	I can only repair it temporarily.
Mobil anda sudah sangat parah.	Your car is beyond repair.
Ini tidak bisa diperbaiki.	It can't be repaired.
Ini akan selesai ...	It will be ready ...
nanti	later today
besok	tomorrow
dalam ...hari	in ... days

DAYS OF THE WEEK ➤ 218; NUMBERS ➤ 216

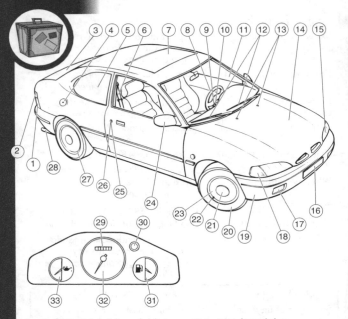

1 taillights [back lights] **lampu belakang**
2 brakelights **lampu rem**
3 trunk [boot] **bagasi**
4 gas tank door [petrol cap]
  penutup tangki bensin
5 window **jendela**
6 seat belt **sabuk pengaman**
7 sunroof **sunroof**
8 steering wheel **setir**
9 ignition **starter**
10 ignition key **kunci kontak**
11 windshield [windscreen] **kaca**
12 windshield [windscreen] wipers **wiper**
13 windshield [windscreen] washer
  pembersih kaca
14 hood [bonnet] **kap mesin**
15 headlights **lampu depan**
16 license [number] plate **pelat nomor**

17 fog lamp **lampu kabut**
18 turn signals [indicators] **lampu sein**
19 fender [bumper] **bumper**
20 tires [tyres] **ban**
21 wheel cover [hubcap] **dop roda**
22 valve **pentil**
23 wheels **roda**
24 outside [wing] mirror **kaca spion**
25 automatic locks [central locking]
  kunci otomatis
26 lock **kunci**
27 wheel rim **pelek roda**
28 exhaust pipe **knalpot**
29 odometer [milometer] **meteran kilometer**
30 warning light **lampu peringatan**
31 fuel gauge **meteran bensin**
32 speedometer **spedometer**
33 oil gauge **meteran oli**

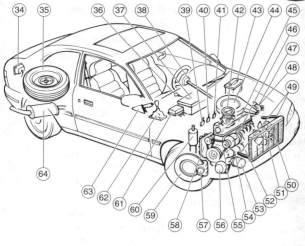

34 backup [reversing] lights
    lampu mundur
35 spare tire **ban cadangan**
36 choke **cok**
37 heater **pemanas**
38 steering column **batang setir**
39 accelerator **pedal**
40 pedal **pedal**
41 clutch **kopling**
42 carburetor **karburator**
43 battery **aki**
44 air filter **saringan udara**
45 camshaft **batang silinder**
46 alternator **alternator**
47 distributor **distributor**
48 points **platina**
49 radiator hose (top/bottom) **selang**
    radiator (atas/bawah)

50 radiator **radiator**
51 fan **kipas angin**
52 engine **mesin**
53 oil filter **saringan oli**
54 starter motor **mesin starter**
55 fan belt **tali kipas**
56 horn **klakson**
57 brake pads **kanvas rem**
58 transmission [gearbox] **kotak**
    persneling
59 brakes **rem**
60 shock absorbers **shockbreakers**
61 fuses **sekering**
62 gear shift [lever]
    pemindah perseneling
63 handbrake **rem tangan**
64 muffler [silencer]
    saringan udara

Accidents Kecelakaan

There has been an accident.	**Telah terjadi kecelakaan.** *tela terjadee cechelaca'an*
It's …	**Itu …** *itoo*
on the highway [motorway]	**di jalan tol** *dee jalan tol*
near …	**dekat …** *decat*
Where's the nearest telephone?	**Dimana telepon terdekat?** *dimana telepon terdecat*
Call …	**Telepon …** *telepon*
an ambulance	**ambulans** *ambulans*
a doctor	**dokter** *docter*
the fire department [brigade]	**pemadam kebakaran** *permadam cebacaran*
the police	**polisi** *polisee*
Help me, please!	**Bisa anda tolong saya!** *bisa anda tolong saya*

Injuries Luka-luka

There are people injured.	**Ada orang yang terluka.** *ada orang yang terluca*
No one is hurt.	**Tidak ada yang luka.** *tidak ada yang luca*
He's seriously injured.	**Dia luka berat.** *dia luca berrat*
She's unconscious.	**Dia tidak sadar.** *dia tidak sadar*
He can't breathe.	**Dia sesak nafas.** *dia sesak nafas*
He can't move.	**Dia tidak bisa bergerak.** *dia tidak bisa bergerrak*
Don't move him.	**Jangan pindahkan dia.** *jangan pindahcan dia*

Legal matters Urusan Hukum

What's your insurance company?	**Apa perusahaan asuransi anda?** *apa perrusaha'an asuransee anda*

What's your name and address?	**Siapa nama anda dan dimana alamat anda?** *siapa nama anda dan dimana alamat anda*	
The car ran into me.	**Mobil itu tabrak saya.** *mobil itoo tabrak saya*	
The car was driving too close.	**Mobil itu terlalu dekat.** *mobil itoo terlaloo decat*	
I was (only) driving … kmph.	**Saya hanya berjalan dengan kecepatan … kilometer per jam.** *saya hanya berjalan dengan cercherpatan … kilometer per jam*	
I'd like an interpreter.	**Saya mau seorang penterjemah.** *saya mow serorang penterjema*	
I didn't see the sign.	**Saya tidak melihat tanda.** *saya tidak melihat tanda*	
This person saw it happen.	**Orang ini melihat kejadian itu.** *orang inee melihat cejadian itoo*	
The license plate [registration] number was …	**Nomor pelat adalah …** *nomor perlat anda*	

Bisa tolong saya lihat … anda?	Can I see your …, please?
surat Ijin mengemudi	driver's license [licence]
kartu asuransi	insurance card
surat tanda nomor kenderaan	vehicle registration
Kapan terjadi?	What time did it happen?
Dimana terjadi?	Where did it happen?
Apa ada orang lain yang terlibat?	Was anyone else involved?
Apa ada saksi?	Are there any witnesses?
Lampu anda tidak menyala.	Your lights aren't working.
Anda harus bayar denda (di tempat).	You'll have to pay a fine (on the spot).

Asking directions Menanyakan Arah

Excuse me, please.	**Permisi.** *permisee*
How do I get to …?	**Bagaimana cara untuk saya pergi ke …?** *bagaimana chara untuk saya pergee ce*
Where's …?	**Dimana …?** *dimana*
Can you show me on the map where I am?	**Bisa anda memperlihatkan di peta dimana saya berada?** *bisa anda mermperlihatcan dee peta dimana saya berrada*
I've lost my way.	**Saya kesasar.** *saya cesasar*
Can you repeat that, please?	**Bisa tolong anda ulangi itu?** *bisa tolong anda ulangee itoo*
More slowly, please.	**Tolong lebih pelan.** *tolong lebi perlan*
Thanks for your help.	**Terimakasih atas pertolongan anda.** *terrima casee atas pertolongan anda*

Traveling by car Melakukan perjalanan dengan mobil.

Is this the right road for …?	**Apa ini jalan yang benar untuk ke …?** *apa inee jalan yang bernar untuk ce*
Is it far?	**Apa itu jauh?** *apa itoo jow*
How far is it to … from here?	**Berapa jauh ke … dari sini?** *berrapa jow ce … daree sinee*
Where does this road lead?	**Menuju kemana jalan ini?** *menujoo cemana jalan inee*

– Permisi, tolong. Bagaimana cara saya ke stasiun kereta api?
(Excuse me, please. How do I get to the train station?)

– *Ambil belokan kanan yang ketiga lalu terus.*
(*Take the third right and it's straight ahead.*)

– Belokan kanan ketiga. Apa itu jauh?
(Third on the right. Is it far?)

– *Lima meni berjalan kakit.* (*It's 5 minutes on foot.*)

– Terimakasih atas bantuan anda. (Thanks for your help.)

– *Kembali.* (*You're welcome.*)

Location Lokasi

Itu ...	It's ...
terus	straight ahead
di sebelah kiri/kanan	on the left/right
di ujung jalan	at the end of the street
di sudut	on the corner
di sekitar sini	around the corner
diseberang .../di belakang ...	opposite .../behind ...
di samping .../setelah ...	next to .../after ...
Pergi menuju ...	Go down the ...
jalan kecil/jalan utama	side street/main street
Menyeberang ...	Cross the ...
lapangan/jembatan	square/bridge
Ambil belokan ketiga.	Take the third right.
Belok kiri ...	Turn left ...
setelah lampu lalu lintas pertama	after the first traffic light
di persimpangan kedua	at the second intersection

By car Dengan mobil

Itu di sebelah ... dari sini.	It's ... of here.
utara/selatan	north/south
timur/barat	east/west
Ambil jalan ke ...	Take the road for ...
Anda salah jalan.	You're on the wrong road.
Anda harus kembali ke ...	You'll have to go back to ...
Ikuti tanda ke ...	Follow the signs for ...

How far? Seberapa jauh?

Itu ...	It's ...
dekat/jauh	close/a long way
lima menit berjalan kaki	5 minutes on foot
sepuluh menit dengan mobil	10 minutes by car
sekitar seratus meter dari sini	about 100 meters down the road

TIME ➤ *220; NUMBERS* ➤ *216*

Road signs Mar jalan

PERALIHAN JALAN	detour [diversion]
JALAN SATU ARAH	one-way street
JALAN DITUTUP	road closed
KAWASAN SEKOLAH	school zone [path]
STOP	stop
TIDAK BOLEH MEMOTONG JALAN	no passing [overtaking]
JALAN PELAN-PELAN	drive slowly
GUNAKAN LAMPU DEPAN	use headlights

Town plans Tata kota

lapangan terbang	airport
bank	bank
rute bis	bus route
setopan bis	bus stop
gereja	church
pusat perbelanjaan	department store
rumah sakit	hospital
pusat informasi	information office
bioskop	movie theater [cinema]
taman	park
tempat parkir	parking lot [car park]
penyeberangan jalan	pedestrian crossing
kawasan pejalan kaki	pedestrian zone [precinct]
kantor polisi	police station
kantor pos	post office
lapangan bermain	playing field [sports ground]
sekolah	school
stasiun kereta api	train station
stadion	stadium
antrian taksi	taxi stand [rank]
teater	theater
Anda berada di sini.	You are here.

DICTIONARY ➤ 169; SIGHTSEEING ➤ 97–107

Sightseeing

Tourist information office
Kantor Penerangan Wisata

Where's the tourist office?	**Dimanakah kantor penerangan wisata?** *dimanaca cantor pernerrangan wisata*
What are the main points of interest?	**Dimanakah tempat-tempat utama yang menarik?** *dimanaca tempat tempat utama yang mernarik*
We're here for …	**Kami di sini untuk …** *camee dee sinee untuk*
a few hours	**beberapa jam** *berberapa jam*
a day	**satu hari** *satoo haree*
a week	**satu minggu** *satoo minggoo*
Can you recommend …?	**Bisakah anda sarankan …?** *bisaca anda sarankan*
a sightseeing tour	**jalan-jalan lihat pemandangan** *jalan jalan lihat pemandangan*
an excursion	**darmawisata** *darmawisata*
a boat trip	**pesiar dengan kapal** *persiar dengan capal*
Do you have any information on …?	**Apakah anda punya informasi tentang …?** *apaca anda punya informasee tentang*
Are there any trips to …?	**Adakah wisata ke …?** *adaca wisata ce*

Excursions Darmawisata

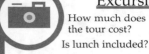

How much does the tour cost?	**Berapa biaya untuk wisata itu?** *berrapa biaya untuk wisata itoo*
Is lunch included?	**Apakah termasuk makan siang?** *apaca termasuk makan siang*
Where do we leave from?	**Darimana kita berangkat?** *darimana cita berrangkat*
What time does the tour start?	**Pukul berapa perjalanan dimulai?** *pucul berrapa perjalanan dimulay*
What time do we get back?	**Pukul berapa kita kembali?** *pucul berrapa cita cembalee*
Do we have free time in …?	**Apakah ada waktu bebas di …?** *apaca ada wactoo bebas dee*
Is there an English-speaking guide?	**Apakah ada pemandu wisata berbahasa Inggris?** *apaca ada pemandoo wisata berbahasa Inggris*

On the tour Dalam perjalanan wisata

Are we going to see …?	**Apakah kita akan pergi melihat …?** *apaca cita acan pergee melihat*
We'd like to have a look at the …	**Kami ingin melihat …** *camee ingin melihat*
Can we stop here …?	**Bisakah kita berhenti di sini …?** *bisaca cita berhentee dee sinee*
to take photographs	**untuk ambil foto** *untuk ambil foto*
to buy souvenirs	**untuk beli suvenir** *untuk beli suvenir*
to use the restrooms [toilets]	**untuk ke kamar kecil** *untuk ce camar cechil*
Would you take a photo of us, please?	**Maukah anda menolong mengambil foto kami?** *mowca anda tolong ambil foto camee*
How long do we have in …?	**Berama lama kita di sini …?** *berrapa lama cita dee sinee*
Wait! … isn't back yet.	**Tunggu! … belum kembali.** *tunggoo! … berlum cermbalee*

Sights Pemandangan

Where's the …?	**Dimanakah … nya?**
	dimanaca … nya
art gallery	**galeri seni** *galeree sernee*
botanical garden	**kebun raya** *cerbun raya*
castle	**kastil** *castil*
cathedral	**gereja katedral** *gerreja catedral*
cemetery	**kuburan** *cuburan*
church	**gereja** *gerreja*
downtown area	**daerah pusat kota**
	daera pusat cota
fountain	**air mancur** *air manchur*
historic site	**tempat bersejarah** *tempat bersejara*
market	**pasar** *pasar*
(war) memorial	**tugu peringatan (perang)**
	tugoo peringatan (perrang)
monastery	**biara** *biara*
museum	**museum** *museum*
old town	**kota tua** *cota tua*
opera house	**gedung opera** *gedung opera*
palace	**istana** *istana*
park	**taman** *taman*
parliament building	**gedung parlemen** *gerdung parlermen*
ruins	**reruntuhan** *rerruntuhan*
shopping area	**pusat perbelanjaan**
	pusat perbelanja'an
statue	**patung** *patung*
theater	**teater** *teater*
tower	**menara** *mernara*
town hall	**balai kota** *balay cota*
viewing point	**tempat lihat pemandangan**
	tempat lihat pemandangan
Can you show me on the map?	**Bisakah anda menunjukkan saya dimana di peta?** *bisaca anda tunjukkan saya dimana dee perta*

DIRECTIONS ➤ 94

Admission Karcis Masuk

Is the … open to the public?	**Apakah … dibuka untuk umum?** *apaca … dibuca untuk umum*
What are the hours?	**Pukul berapa jam bukanya?** *pucul berrapa jam bukanya*
When does it close?	**Pukul berapa tutupnya?** *pucul berrapa jam tutupnya*
Is … open on Sundays?	**Apakah … buka pada hari Minggu?** *apaca … buca pada haree minggoo*
When's the next guided tour?	**Kapan wisata dengan pemandu wisata yang berikutnya?** *capan wisata dengan permandoo wisata yang berrikutnya*
Do you have a guide book (in English)?	**Apakah anda punya buku panduan (dalam bahasa Inggris)?** *apaca anda punya bucu panduan (dalam bahasa Inggris)*
Can I take photos?	**Bisakah ambil foto?** *bisaca ambil foto*
Is there access for the disabled?	**Apakah ada sarana untuk orang cacat?** *apaca ada sarana untuk orang chachat*

Paying/Tickets Pembayaran/Karcis

… tickets, please.	**… mohon karcisnya.** *mohon carchisnya*
How much is the entrance fee?	**Berapa karcis masuknya?** *berrapa carchis masuknya*
Are there any discounts for …?	**Apakah ada potongan untuk …?** *apaca ada potongan untuk*
children/groups	**anak-anak/rombongan** *anak anak/rombongan*
senior citizens/students	**orang tua/pelajar** *orang tua/perlajar*
the disabled	**orang cacat** *orang chachat*
One adult and two children, please.	**Tolong satu dewasa dan dua anak-anak.** *tolong satoo dewasa dan dua anak anak*

> – Tolong lima tiket. Apakah ada potongan?
> (Five tickets, please. Are there
> any discounts?)
> – Ya. Anak-anak dan pensiunan
> seribu rupiah. *(Yes. Children and
> senior citizens are one thousand rupiah.)*
> – Tolong dua dewasa dan tiga anak-anak.
> (Two adults and three children, please.)
> – Semuanya enam ribu rupiah.
> (That's six thousand rupiah, please.)

BEBAS MASUK	free admission
BUKA/UTUP	open/closed
TOKO CENDERAMATA	gift shop
JAM MASUK TERAKHIR PUKUL LIMA SORE	last entry at 5 p.m.
TUR BERIKUT JAM …	next tour at …
DILARANG MASUK	no entry
DILARANG PAKAI (ALAT) KILAT	no flash photography
DILARANG MENGAMBIL FOTO	no photography
JAM KUNJUNGAN	hours [visiting hours]

Impressions Kesan-kesan

It's …	**Itu …** *itoo*
amazing	**mengagumkan** *merngagumcan*
beautiful	**indah** *inda*
boring	**membosankan** *mermbosancan*
interesting	**menarik** *mernarik*
romantic	**romantis** *romantis*
strange	**aneh** *ane*
superb	**hebat** *hebat*
terrible	**buruk sekali** *buruk serkalee*
ugly	**jelek** *jelek*
I like it.	**Saya suka itu.** *saya suca itoo*
I don't like it.	**Saya tidak suka itu.** *saya tidak suca itoo*

101

Tourist glossary
Istilah pariwisata

air terjun waterfalls

arsitektur architecture

barang antik antiques

barang barang kulit leather goods

barang barang perak silverware

batik batik

candi ancient Hindu temple

gamelan Javanese orchestra

istana palace

kain textiles

kaligrafi calligraphy

kebun raya botanical garden

kerajinan tangan handicrafts

keramik ceramics/pottery

keraton sultan's palace

keroncong popular music

lukisan painting

mesjid mosque

museum museum

pantai beach

patung dewa statue of gods

patung sculpture

pura Hindu temple

ruangan utama main hall

seni art

seni pahat sculpture

seni visual visual art

taman hiburan recreational park

tempat bersejarah historical site

tenunan tangan handwoven cloth

tugu nasional national monument

ukiran kayu woodcrafts

wayang golek wooden puppet show

wayang kulit leather puppet show

wayang orang Javanese stage play

Who?/What?/When?
Siapa?/Apa?/Kapan?

What's that building?	**Itu gedung apa?** _itoo gedung apa_
When was it built?	**Kapan itu dibangun?** _capan itoo dibangun_
Who was the artist/architect?	**Siapa senimannya/arsiteknya?** _siapa sernimannya/arsiteknya_
What style is that?	**Gaya apakah itu?** _gaya apaca itoo_
What period is that?	**Pada jaman apakah itu?** _pada jaman apaca itoo_

7th century

The Sumatran Hindu-Buddhist kingdom of Sriwijaya conducted substantial international trade, which was run by Tamils and Chinese. The empire had declined by the 12th century and was replaced by smaller kingdoms.

13th century

Majapahit, founded in 1294, was one of the greatest of Indonesian states and the last Hindu kingdom. Under the reign of Hayam Wuruk, the state gained control over much of the archipelago. After his death, the kingdom declined rapidly.

15–17th centuries

Arab traders had established settlements in the 7th century. The first Muslim inscriptions found in Java date from the 11th century. By the time of the Majapahit state's final collapse, many of its old satellite kingdoms had declared themselves independent Muslim states.

By the 15th century the center of power had moved to the Malay peninsula and the trading kingdom of Melaka. The Portuguese captured Melaka in 1511. Their control of strategic trading ports, such as Melaka, Goa, and Macau, was based on their fortified bases and superior firepower at sea. Soon other European nations sent ships, notably the Spanish, Dutch, and English. It was the Dutch who eventually laid the foundations of the Indonesian state of today.

Places of worship
Tempat-tempat bersembahyang

Catholic/ Protestant church	**Gereja katolik/protestan/kristen** *gererjah katalik/protestan/kristern*
mosque	**masjid** *masjid*
synagogue	**sinagog** *sinagog*
temple	**kuil/pura** *cuil/poora*
Buddhist temple	**kuil Buda** *cuil booda*

Religion and culture

Indonesia is made up of a wide spectrum of societies and cultures. In recent times, mass education, mass media, and a government policy of Indonesian national identity – including the promotion of Bahasa Indonesia (the Indonesian language) – have created a definite Indonesian identity.

Indonesia is predominantly Islamic but in many parts Islam has become fused with traditional customs and with Hindu-Buddhism, making it appear very different from the orthodox Middle Eastern religion. Christianity and animism are widespread, and in Bali they practice a unique form of Hinduism. The Chinese section of the population is mainly Buddhist.

Despite the changes that the modern age has brought, Indonesia remains one of the most traditional countries of South-East Asia. The extended family is the traditional core of society and beyond this the main social unit is the village.

Indonesia is a nation of many opposing forces: orthodox Islam versus local Islam, Islam versus Christianity versus Hinduism, country versus city, modern versus traditional, rich versus poor, and inner parts of the country versus the outer parts. Although it might be wise to avoid East Timor, Aceh, and Irian Jaya because of the recent troubles, Indonesia is a unique and beautiful country with much to see and do.

In the countryside
Di daerah pedesaan

I'd like a map of …	**Saya mau peta …** *saya mow peta*
this region	**wilayah ini** *wilaya inee*
walking routes	**rute jalan kaki** *rute jalan caci*
cycle routes	**rute sepeda** *rute serpeda*
How far is it to …?	**Berapa jauh ke …?** *berrapa jaowh ce*
Is there a trail/scenic route to …?	**Apakah ada rute jalan kecil/ berpemandangan indah ke …?** *apaca ada rute jalan cechil/ berpemandangan inda ce*
Can you show me on the map?	**Bisakah anda tunjukkan saya di peta?** *bisaca anda tunjukkan saya dee peta*
I'm lost.	**Saya kesasar.** *saya cesasar*
Can you show me on the map where I am?	**Bisa anda memperlihatkan di peta dimana saya berada?** *bisa anda mermperlihatcan dee peta dimana saya berrada*
Can you repeat that, please?	**Bisa tolong anda ulangi itu?** *bisa tolong anda ulangee itoo*
More slowly, please.	**Tolong lebih pelan.** *tolong lebi perlan*
Thanks for your help.	**Terimakasih atas pertolongan anda.** *terrima casee atas pertolongan anda*

Organized walks Wisata jalan kaki

When does the guided walk start?	**Kapan wisata jalan kaki dengan pemandu dimulai?** _capan wisata jalan caci dengan pemandoo dimulay_
When will we return?	**Kapan kita akan kembali?** _capan cita acan cermbalee_
Is it a … course?	**Apakah itu jalan …?** _apaca itoo jalan_
gentle/medium/tough	**santai/biasa/banyak tantangan** _santay/biasa/banyak tantangan_
I'm exhausted.	**Saya capai.** _saya chapay_
How long are we resting here?	**Berapa lama kita istirahat di sini?** _berrapa lama cita istirahat dee sinee_
What kind of … is that?	**Jenis … apakah itu?** _jenis … apaca itoo_
animal	**binatang** _binatang_
bird	**burung** _burung_
flower	**bunga** _bunga_
tree	**pohon** _pohon_

Geographic features Ciri-ciri Geografis

beach	**pantai** _pantay_
bridge	**jembatan** _jembatan_
canal	**kanal** _canal_
cave	**gua** _gua_
cliff	**jurang** _jurang_
farm	**pertanian** _pertanian_
field	**ladang** _ladang_

HIKING GEAR ➤ 145

footpath	**jalan setapak** _jalan setapak_
forest	**hutan** _hutan_
hill	**bukit** _bukit_
lake	**danau** _danow_
mountain	**gunung** _gunung_
mountain pass	**jalan pegunungan** _jalan pegunungan_
mountain range	**jajaran pegunungan** _jajaran pegunungan_
nature reserve	**cadangan alam** _chadangan alam_
panorama	**pemandangan** _permandangan_
park	**taman** _taman_
peak	**puncak** _punchak_
picnic area	**tempat piknik** _tempat picnik_
pond	**kolam** _colam_
rapids	**riam** _riam_
river	**sungai** _sungay_
sea	**laut** _lowt_
stream	**sungai kecil** _sungay cechil_
valley	**lembah** _lembah_
viewpoint	**tempat melihat pemandangan** _tempat melihat permandangan_
village	**kampung** _campung_
waterfall	**air terjun** _air terjun_
wood	**hutan kecil** _hutan cechil_

Leisure

Events Acara

Do you have a program of events?	**Apakah anda punya program acara?** _apaca anda punya program achara_
Can you recommend a ...?	**Bisakah anda sarankan sebuah ...?** _bisaca anda sarankan sebua_
ballet	**balet** _balet_
concert	**konser** _conser_
movie [film]	**film** _film_
opera	**opera** _opera_
play	**sandiwara** _sandiwara_

Availability Ketersediaan

When does it start?	**Kapan dimulai?** _capan dimulay_
When does it end?	**Kapan berakhir?** _capan berakhir_
Are there any seats for tonight?	**Apakah ada tempat untuk malam ini?** _apaca ada tempat untuk malam inee_
Where can I get tickets?	**Dimana saya bisa dapat karcis?** _dimana saya bisa dapat carchis_
There are ... of us.	**Kami ada ... orang.** _camee ada ... orang_

Tickets Karcis

How much are the seats? **Berapa harga karcisnya?** *berrapa harga carchisnya*

I'd like two tickets for tonight's concert. **Saya mau dua karcis untuk konser malam ini.** *saya mow dua carchis untuk conser malam inee*

I'd like to reserve … **Saya mau pesan …** *saya mow pesan*

three tickets for Sunday evening **tiga karcis untuk Minggu malam** *tiga carchis untuk minggoo malam*

one ticket for the Friday matinée **satu karcis untuk Jumat siang** *satoo carchis untuk jumat siang*

Can I pay by credit card? **Bisakah saya bayar dengan kartu kredit?** *bisaca saya bayar dengan cartoo credit*

May I have a program, please? **Bisa saya dapat program acara?** *bisa saya dapat program acara*

Where's the coatcheck [cloakroom]? **Dimana tempat penitipan?** *dimana tempat pernitipan*

– Bisakah saya bantu anda? (Can I help you?)
– Tolong saya mau dua tiket untuk konser malam ini.
  (I'd like two tickets for tonight's concert, please.)
– Baik. (Certainly.)
– Bisakah saya bayar dengan kartu kredit?
  (Can I pay by credit card?)
– Ya. (Yes.)
– Kalau begitu saya bayar pakai Visa.
  (In that case I'll pay by Visa.)
– Terimakasih. Tolong tanda tangan di sini.
  (Thank you. Sign here, please.)

KARCIS HABIS	sold out
KARCIS UNTUK HARI INI	tickets for today
PEMESANAN AWAL	advance reservations

NUMBERS ➤ 216

Movies [Cinema] Bioskop

In Indonesia, all foreign movies are subtitled.

Is there a movie theater [cinema] near here?	**Adakah ada bioskop di dekat sini?** *apaca ada bioscop dee dekat sinee*
What's playing at the movies [on at the cinema] tonight?	**Apa yang sedang main di bioskop malam ini?** *apa yang sedang main dee bioscop malam inee*
Is the film in the original English?	**Apakah filmnya dalam bahasa Inggris?** *apaca filmnya dalam bahasa inggris*
A …, please.	**Tolong satu …** *tolong satoo*
box [carton] of popcorn	**kotak popcorn** *cotak popcorn*
chocolate ice cream [choc-ice]	**es krim coklat** *es crim choclat*
hot dog	**hot dog**
soft drink	**minuman ringan** *minuman ringan*
small/regular/large	**kecil/biasa/besar** *cechil/biasa/bersar*

Theater Teater

What's playing at the TIM Theater?	**Apa yang main di Teater TIM?** *apa yang main dee TIM teater*
Who's the playwright?	**Siapa penulis naskahnya?** *siapa penulis nascanya*
Do you think I'd enjoy it?	**Apakah menurut anda saya akan suka?** *apaca menurut anda saya acan suca*
I don't know much Indonesian.	**Saya sangat sedikit (bisa) mengerti bahasa Indonesia.** *saya sangat serdikit (bisa) mengerti bahasa indonesia*

Opera/Ballet/Dance
Opera/Balet/Tari

Where's the theater?	**Dimanakan teaternya?** *dimanaca teaternya*
Who is the composer/ soloist?	**Siapa penciptanya/pemain tunggalnya?** *siapa pernchiptanya/ permain tunggalnya*
Who's dancing?	**siapa penarinya?** *siapa pernarinya*
I'm interested in contemporary dance.	**Saya tertarik pada tari kontemporer.** *saya tertarik pada taree contemporer*

Music/Concerts Musik/Konser

Where's the concert hall?	**Dimanakah tempat konser musik?** *dimanaca tempat conser musik*
Which orchestra/band is playing?	**Orkestra/band apa yang main?** *orcestra/band apa yang main*
What are they playing?	**Apa yang mereka mainkan?** *apa yang merreca maincan*
Who is the conductor/ soloist?	**Siapa konduktorny/pemain tunggalnya?** *siapa conductor/ permain tunggalnya*
Who is the support band?	**Siapa band pendukungnya?** *siapa band perndukungnya*
I really like …	**Saya sangat suka …** *saya sangat suca*
folk music	**musik rakyat** *musik racyat*
jazz	**jazz** *jaz*
music of the sixties	**musik tahun 60-an** *musik tahun enampuluhan*
pop/rock music	**musik pop/rock** *musik pop/rok*
soul music	**musik soul** *musik soul*
Are they popular?	**Apakah mereka terkenal?** *apaca merreca tercenal*

Nightlife Kehidupan malam

What is there to do in the evenings?	**Apa yang bisa dilakukan di sana pada malam hari?** *apa yang bisa dilacucan dee sana pada malam haree*
Can you recommend/suggest a …?	**Bisakah anda sarankan/usulkan suatu …?** *bisaca anda sarankan/usulcan suatu*
Is there a …?	**Apakah di sana ada …?** *apaca dee sana ada*
bar/restaurant	**bar/restoran** *bar/restoran*
cabaret	**kabaret** *cabare*
casino	**kasino** *casino*
discotheque	**diskotek** *discotek*
nightclub	**klub malam** *club malam*
What type of music do they play?	**Jenis musik apa yang mereka mainkan?** *jenis musik apa yang merreca mainkan*
How do I get there?	**Bagaimana caranya saya ke sana?** *bagaimana charanya saya ce sana*
Is there an admission charge?	**Apakah ada karcis masuknya?** *apaca ada carchis masuknya*

Admission Karcis masuk

What time does the show start?	**Jam berapakah pertunjukan mulai?** *jam berrapaca pertunjukkan mulay*
Is there a cover charge?	**Apakah ada karcis masuk?** *apaca ada carchis masuk*
Are reservations necessary?	**Apakah perlu pesan karcis sebelumnya?** *apaca perloo pesan carchis serbelumnya*
Can you have dinner there?	**Bisakah makan malam di sana?** *bisaca makan malam dee sana*
I'd like a good table.	**Saya mau meja yang baik.** *saya mow meja yang baik*

Children Anak-anak

Can you recommend something for the children? | **Bisakah anda sarankan sesuatu untuk anak-anak?** _bisaca anda sarankan sesuatu untuk anak anak_

Are there changing facilities here for babies? | **Apakah ada tempat ganti popok untuk bayi disini?** _apaca ada tem pat ganti popok untuk bayee disinee_

Where are the restrooms [toilets]? | **Dimanakah kamar kecil?** _dimanaca camar cechil_

fairground | **pekan raya** _pecan raya_

kiddie [paddling] pool | **kolam renang anak-anak** _colam rernang anak anak_

playground | **taman bermain** _taman bermain_

zoo | **kebun binatang** _kerbun binatang_

Babysitting Menjaga anak

Can you recommend a reliable babysitter? | **Bisakah anda menyarankan penjaga anak yang bisa dipercaya?** _bisaca anda sarankan pernjaga anak yang bisa diperchaya_

Is there constant supervision? | **Apaca pengawasannya terus merus?** _apakah pengawasannya terus menerus_

When can I bring them? | **Kapan mereka bisa saya bawa?** _capan merreca bisa saya bawa_

I'll pick them up at … | **Saya akan jemput mereka pada …** _saya acan jemput merreca pada_

She's 3, and he's 18 months. | **Yang perempuan berumur tiga tahun, yang laki-laki berumur delapan belas bulan.** _yang perempuan berumur tiga tahun yang laci laci berumur delapan belas bulan_

Sports Olahraga

Spectator sports Menonton

Some of Indonesia's live spectator sports are all-male affairs and can involve illegal gambling. Such 'spectacles' include horseracing, cock fighting, and bull racing.

However, soccer (**sepakbola**) and badminton are the national sports and are followed fanatically. Volleyball is very popular and is played everywhere. A game unique to South-East Asia is **sepak takraw** or **sepak raga** – a cross between volleyball and soccer – is also very popular. **Pencak silat**, Indonesia's own form of martial art is popular in West Java and West Sumatra.

Is there a soccer [football] game [match] this Saturday?	**Apakah ada pertandingan sepakbola Hari Sabtu ini?** _apaca ada pertandingan sepakbola haree sabtoo inee_
Which teams are playing?	**Tim apa yang bermain?** _tim apa yang bermain_
Can you get me a ticket?	**Bisakah anda mendapatkan karcis untuk saya?** _bisaca anda dapatkan carchis untuk saya_
What's the admission charge?	**Berapa karcis masuknya?** _berrapa carchis masuknya_
Where's the racetrack [racecourse]?	**Dimana lintasan pacuan kudanya?** _dimana lintasan pachuan cudanya_
athletics	**atletik** _atletik_
basketball	**bola basket** _bola basket_
cycling	**balap sepeda** _balap serpeda_
golf	**golf** _golf_
horseracing	**pacuan kuda** _pachuan cuda_
soccer [football]	**sepak bola** _serpak bola_
swimming	**berenang** _berrenang_
tennis	**tenis** _tenis_
volleyball	**bola voli** _bola volee_

Participation sports Bermain

Is there a … nearby?	**Apakah ada … di sekitar sini?** _apaca ada … dee secitar sinee_
golf course	**lapangan golf** _lapangan golf_
sports club	**klub olahraga** _club olaraga_
Are there any tennis courts?	**Apakah ada lapangan tenis?** _apaca ada lapangan tenis_
What's the charge per …?	**Berapa biayanya per …?** _berrapa biayanya per_
day/round/hour	**hari/babak/jam** _haree/babak/jam_
Do I need to be a member?	**Apakah saya harus menjadi anggota?** _apaca saya harus mern jadee anggota_
Where can I rent …?	**Dimana saya bisa sewa …?** _dimana saya bisa sewa_
clubs	**klub** _club_
equipment	**peralatan** _peralatan_
a racket	**raket** _racet_
Can I get lessons?	**Bisakah saya ambil les?** _bisaca saya ambil les_
Do you have a fitness room?	**Apakah ada pusat kebugaran?** _apaca ada pusat cebugaran_

I'm sorry, we're booked.	**Maaf, kami penuh.**
There is a deposit of …	**Harus bayar uang muka sebanyak …**
What size are you?	**Berapa ukuran anda?**
You need a passport-size photo.	**Anda perlu foto ukuran paspor.**

RUANG GANTI	changing rooms
HANYA UNTUK ANGGOTA	members only

At the beach Di pantai

Is the beach pebbly/sandy?	**Apakah pantainya berkerikil/ berpasir?** _apaca pantainya berkerikil/berpasir_
Is there a … here?	**Apakah di sini ada …?** _apaca dee sinee ada_
children's pool	**kolam renang anak-anak** _colam rernang untuk anak anak_
swimming pool	**kolam renang** _colam rernang_
indoor/outdoor	**diluar/terbuka** _diluar/terbuca_
Is it safe to swim/ dive here?	**Apakah disini aman untuk berenang?** _apaca dee sinee aman untuk berrenang_
Is it safe for children?	**Apakah aman untuk anak-anak?** _apaca aman untuk anak anak_
Is there a lifeguard?	**Apakah ada pengawal renang?** _apaca ada pengawal rernang_
I want to rent a/some …	**Saya ingin sewa satu/beberapa …** _saya ingin sewa satoo/berberapa_
deck chair	**kursi pantai** _cursi pantai_
jet-ski	**jet-ski** _jet sci_
motorboat	**motorboat** _motorboat_
umbrella [sunshade]	**payung** _payung_
water skis	**papan ski air** _papan sci air_
For … hours.	**Untuk … jam.** _untuk … jam_
What's the charge per day/hour?	**Berapa biayanya per hari/jam?** _berrapa biayanya per haree/jam_

116

Diving and surfing
Menyelam dan selancar

Indonesia is a country of islands and there is plenty of coral. There are many good diving possibilities. Bali has the best-established dive operators that can be found at the main resorts and hotels. Bring your scuba certification with you – most of the main qualifications are recognized. The wet season, which runs from about October to April, is not the best time for diving as storms tend to reduce underwater visibility.

Indonesia has become a popular destination for surfers from all over the world. Nowadays, especially in Bali, crowding can be a problem. Traditionally the best season is between June and August, but it is possible to find good waves outside this period and enjoy less crowding at the same time.

Is the coral good here?	**Apakah batu karangnya bagus disini?** _apaca batoo carangnya bagus disinee_
Is this a good surfing beach?	**Apakah pantainya bagus untuk selancar?** _apaca pantainya bagus untuk serlanchar_
Is there a dive shop near here?	**Apakah ada toko peralatan menyelam disini?** _apaca ada toco perralatan mernyelam disinee_
Is it safe to surf/ dive here?	**Apakah disini aman untuk selancar/ menyelam?** _apaca dee sinee aman untuk serlanchar/menyelam_
I want to rent a/some …	**Saya ingin sewa satu/beberapa …** _saya ingin sewa satoo/berberapa_
wet suit	**pakaian selam** _pacaian serlam_
snorkel	**senorkel** _sernorcel serlanchar_
diving equipment	**peralatan selam** _peralatan selam_
surfboard	**papan selancar** _papan serlanchar_
Can I get surfing/ diving lessons?	**Apakah saya bisa kursus selancar/ menyelam?** _apaca saya bisa cursus serlanchar/mernyelam_

117

Making friends Berteman

Introductions Perkenalan

It is customary for both men and women to shake hands on greeting and introduction.

Hello, we haven't met.	**Hallo, kita belum berkenalan.** *halo, cita berlum berkenalan*
My name's …	**Nama saya …** *nama saya*
May I introduce …	**Bolehkah saya memperkenalkan …** *boleca saya memperkenalcan*
Pleased to meet you.	**Senang bertemu anda.** *sernang bertemu anda*
What's your name?	**Siapakah nama anda?** *siapaca nama anda*
How are you?	**Apa kabarnya?** *apa cabarnya*
Fine, thanks. And you?	**Baik, terimakasih. Dan anda?** *baik terrima casi. dan anda*

> – *Hallo, apa kabarnya?* (Hello, how are you?)
> – *Baik, terimakasih. Dan anda?*
> (Fine, thanks. And you?)
> – *Baik, terimakasih.* (Fine, thanks.)

Where are you from?
Anda berasal dari mana?

Where are you from?	**Anda berasal dari mana?** *anda berrasal daree mana*
Where were you born?	**Anda lahir dimana?** *anda lahir dimana*
I'm from …	**Saya berasal dari …** *saya berrasal daree*
Australia	**Australia** *owstralia*
Britain	**Inggris** *inggris*

118

Canada	**Kanada** _canada_
England	**Inggris** _inggris_
Ireland	**Irlandia** _irlandia_
Scotland	**Skotlandia** _scotlandia_
U.S.	**Amerika Serikat** _america serricat_
Wales	**Wales** _wels_
Where do you live?	**Dimana anda tinggal?** _dimana anda tinggal_
What part of Indonesia are you from?	**Dari Indonesia bagian mana anda berasal?** _daree indonesia bagian mana anda berrasal_
Malaysia	**Malaysia** _malaysia_
Singapore	**Singapura** _singapura_
Philippine	**Filipina** _filipina_
We come here every year.	**Kami datang ke sini setiap tahun.** _camee datang ce sinee setiap tahun_
It's my/our first visit.	**Ini kunjungan pertama saya/kami.** _inee kunjungan pertama saya/camee_
Have you ever been to …?	**Apakah anda pernah ke …?** _apaca anda perna ce_
the U.K./U.S.	**Inggris/Amerika Serikat** _inggris/america serricat_
Do you like it here?	**Apakah anda suka di sini?** _apaca anda suca dee sinee_
What do you think of the …?	**Bagaimana pendapat anda tentang …?** _bagaimana perndapat anda tentang_
I love the … here.	**Saya suka … di sini** _saya suca … dee sinee_
I don't really like the … here.	**Saya tidak terlalu suka dengan … di sini** _saya tidak terlaloo suca dengan … dee sinee_
food/people	**makanan/orang** _macanan/orang_

Who are you with?
Dengan siapakah anda?

Who are you with?	**Dengan siapakah anda?** *dengan siapaca anda*
I'm on my own.	**Saya sendirian.** *saya serndirian*
I'm with a friend.	**Saya dengan seorang teman.** *saya dengan seorang teman*
I'm with my ...	**Saya dengan ... saya.** *saya dengan ... saya*
husband/wife	**suami/isteri** *suamee/isterree*
family	**keluarga** *celuarga*
children/parents	**anak-anak/orang tua** *anak anak/orang tua*
boyfriend/girlfriend	**teman laki-laki/teman wanita** *teman lacee lacee/teman wanita*
father/son/brother	**ayah/anak laki-laki/saudara laki-laki** *aya/anak lacee lacee/saudara lacee lacee*
mother/daughter/sister	**ibu/anak perempuan/saudara perempuan** *iboo/anak perrempuan/saudara perrempuan*
What's your son's/wife's name?	**Siapa nama anak laki-laki/isteri anda?** *siapa nama anak lacee lacee/isterree anda*
Are you married?	**Apakah anda sudah menikah?** *apaca anda suda menica*
I'm ...	**Saya ...** *saya ...*
married/single	**sudah menikah/masih bujangan** *suda menica/masi bujangan*
divorced/separated	**bercerai/berpisah** *bercheray/berpisa*
engaged	**sudah bertunangan** *suda bertunangan*
Do you have any children?	**Apakah anda punya anak?** *apaca anda punya anak*

What do you do? Apa pekerjaan anda?

What do you do?	**Apa pekerjaan anda?** _apa perkerjaan anda_
What are you studying?	**Apa belajar di bidang apa?** _apa berlajar dee bidang apa_
I'm studying …	**Saya belajar …** _saya berlajar_
I'm in …	**Saya usaha bidang …** _saya usaha bidang_
business	**bisnis** _bisnis_
engineering	**perekayasan** _perrecayasan_
sales	**penjualan** _pernjualan_
Who do you work for …?	**Anda bekerja di mana …?** _anda berkerja dee mana_
I work for …	**Saya bekerja di …** _saya berkerja dee_
I'm (a/an) …	**Saya …** _saya_
accountant	**akuntan** _acuntan_
housewife	**ibu rumah tangga** _iboo ruma tangga_
student	**pelajar** _perlajar_
retired	**pensiunan** _pernsiunan_
self-employed	**wiraswastawan** _wiraswastawan_
between jobs	**pekerja sambilan** _perkerja sambilan_
What are your interests/ hobbies?	**Apa kegemaran/hobby anda?** _apa cegemaran/hobi anda_
I like …	**Saya suka …** _saya suca_
music	**musik** _musik_
reading	**membaca** _membacha_
sports	**olahraga** _olaraga_
I play …	**Saya bermain …** _saya bermain_

What weather! Wah cuacanya!

What a lovely day!	**Wah hari yang indah!** _wa haree yang inda_
What terrible weather!	**Wah cuacanya buruk!** _wa chuachanya buruk_
It's hot/cold today.	**Hari ini panas/dingin.** _haree inee panas/dingin_
Is it usually this warm?	**Apakah biasanya sepanas ini?** _apaca biasanya serpanas inee_
Do you think it's going to … tomorrow?	**Menurut anda apakah besok …** _menurut anda apaca besok_
be a nice day	**hari yang baik** _haree yang baik_
rain	**hujan** _hujan_
What is the weather forecast for tomorrow?	**Apa ramalan cuaca untuk besok?** _apa ramalan chuacha untuk besok_
It's …	**Cuacanya …** _chuachanya_
cloudy	**berawan** _berrawan_
foggy	**berkabut** _bercabut_
stormy	**banyak angin keras** _banyak angin ceras_
windy	**berangin** _berrangin_
It's raining.	**Hari hujan.** _haree hujan_
It's sunny.	**Harinya cerah.** _harinya chera_
Has the weather been like this for long?	**Apakah cuaca seperti ini sudah lama?** _apaca chuacha serpertee inee suda lama_
Will it be good weather for windsurfing?	**Akankah cuaca baik untuk selancar angin?** _acanca chuacha baik untuk serlanchar angin_

RAMALAN CUACA weather forecast

Enjoying your trip?
Apakah anda menikmati perjalanannya?

Apakah anda sedang berlibur?	Are you on vacation?
Bagaimana anda sampai ke sini?	How did you get here?
Dimana anda menginap?	Where are you staying?
Sudah berapa lama anda di sini?	How long have you been here?
Berapa lama anda menginap?	How long are you staying?
Apa yang sejauh ini sudah anda lakukan?	What have you done so far?
Kemana tujuan anda berikutnya?	Where are you going next?
Apakah anda menikmati liburan anda?	Are you enjoying your vacation?

I'm here on … **Saya di sini dalam rangka …** _saya dee sinee dalam rangca_

business **bisnis** _bisnis_

vacation [holiday] **liburan** _liburan_

We came by … **Kami datang dengan …** _camee datang dengan_

train/bus/plane **kereta api/bis/pesawat terbang** _cerreta apee/bis/persawat terbang_

car/ferry (boat) **mobil/ferry** _mobil/feri_

I have a rental car. **Saya punya mobil sewaan.** _saya punya mobil sewa'an_

We're staying in/at … **Kami menginap di …** _camee menginap dee_

a campsite/guesthouse **lokasi perkemahan/sebuah pesanggrahan** _locasee percemahan/ serbua persanggrahan_

a hotel **hotel** _hotel_

Invitations Undangan

Would you like to have dinner with us on …?	**Maukah anda makan malam bersama kami di …?** *mowca anda makan malam bersama camee dee*
Are you free for lunch?	**Apakah anda punya waktu untuk makan siang?** *apaca anda punya wactoo untuk makan siang*
Can you come for a drink this evening?	**Bisakah anda datang malam ini untuk minum-minum?** *bisaca anda datang malam inee untuk minum minum*
We're having a party. Can you come?	**Kami bikin pesta. Bisakah anda datang?** *camee bicin pesta. bisaca anda datang*
May we join you?	**Bolehkah kami bergabung dengan anda?** *boleca camee bergabung dengan anda*
Would you like to join us?	**Maukah anda bergabung dengan kami?** *mowca anda bergabung dengan camee*

Going out Pergi ke luar

What are your plans for …?	**Apa rencana kamu untuk …?** *apa renchana camoo untuk*
today/tonight/tomorrow	**hari ini/malam ini/besok** *haree inee/malam inee/besok*
Are you free this evening?	**Apakah kamu ada waktu malam ini?** *apaca camoo ada wactoo malam inee*
Would you like to …?	**Maukah kamu …?** *mowca camoo*
go dancing	**pergi ke tempat berdansa** *pergee ce tempat berdansa*
go for a drink	**pergi minum-minum** *pergee minum minum*
go out for a meal	**pergi makan** *pergee macan*

124

Accepting/Declining Menerima/Menolak

Thank you. I'd love to.
Terima kasih. Saya mau. *casi. saya mow*

Thank you, but I'm busy.
Terima kasih, tetapi sayang saya sibuk. *terrima casi tertapee sayang saya sibuk*

May I bring a friend?
Bolehkah saya bawa seorang teman? *boleca saya bawa serorang terman*

Where shall we meet?
Dimana sebaiknya kita bertemu? *dimana sebaiknya cita bertemoo*

I'll meet you …
Saya akan bertemu kamu … *saya acan bertemoo camoo*

in front of your hotel
di depan hotel kamu *dee derpan hotel camoo*

I'll call for you at 8.
Saya akan telepon kamu pukul delapan. *saya acan telepon camoo pukul derlapan*

Could we make it a bit earlier/later?
Bisakah kita bertemu lebih awal/lambat. *bisaca cita bertemoo lebi awal/lambat*

How about another day?
Bagaimana kalau hari lain? *bagaimana calow haree lain*

That will be fine.
Boleh saja. *bole saja*

Dining out/in Makan ke luar/di rumah

Let me buy you a drink.
Biar saya yang belikan kamu minuman. *biar saya yang belikan camoo minuman*

Do you like …?
Apakah kamu suka …? *apaca camoo suca*

What are you going to have?
Apa yang kamu mau? *apa yang camoo mow*

That was a lovely meal.
Wah makanannya enak *wa macanannya enak*

Encounters Pertemuan

Do you mind if …?	**Apakah anda keberatan jika …?** *apaca anda ceberatan jica*
I sit here/I smoke	**saya duduk di sini/saya merokok** *saya duduk dee sinee/saya merokok*
Can I get you a drink?	**Bisakah saya pesankan anda minuman?** *bisaca saya pesancan anda minuman*
I'd love to have some company.	**Saya ingin ada yang temani.** *saya ingin ada yang temanee*
Is my Indonesian that bad?	**Apakah Bahasa Indonesia saya demikian buruknya?** *apaca bahasa indonesia saya dermikian buruknya*
Shall we go somewhere quieter?	**Apakah sebaiknya kita pergi ke tempat lain yang lebih tenang?** *apaca serbaicnya cita pergee ce tempat lain yang lebi ternang*
Leave me alone, please!	**Tolong jangan ganggu saya!** *tolong jangan ganggoo saya*
You look great!	**Kamu tampak luar biasa!** *camoo tampak luar biasa*
I'm afraid we've got to leave now.	**Saya rasa kita harus pulang sekarang.** *saya rasa cita harus pulang serkarang*
Thanks for the evening.	**Terimakasih untuk malam ini.** *terrima casi untuk malam inee*
It was great.	**Sangat luar biasa.** *sangat luar biasa*
Can I see you again tomorrow?	**Bisakah saya bertemu kamu lagi besok?** *bisaca saya bertemoo camoo lagee besok*
See you soon.	**Sampai ketemu lagi.** *sampay certemoo lagee*
Can I have your address?	**Bisakah saya minta alamat kamu?** *bisaca saya minta alamat camoo*

Telephoning Bertelepon

The government-run Telkom has offices in many towns and cities. Offices are usually open 24 hours a day. These are the cheapest places to make international or long-distance (**inter-lokal**) calls. They often have fax services too.

Can I have your telephone number?	**Bisakah saya minta nomor telepon kamu?** _bisaca saya minta nomor telepon camoo_
Here's my number.	**Ini nomor saya.** _inee nomor saya_
Please call me.	**Teleponlah saya.** _teleponla saya_
I'll give you a call.	**Saya akan telepon kamu.** _saya acan telepon camoo_
Where's the nearest telephone booth?	**Dimanakah telepon umum terdekat?** _dimanaca telepon umum terdecat_
May I use your phone?	**Bolehkah saya gunakan telepon kamu?** _boleca saya gunacan telepon camoo_
It's an emergency.	**Ini keadaan mendesak.** _inee ceada'an merndesak_
I'd like to call someone in England.	**Saya mau telepon seseorang ke Inggris.** _saya mow telepon seserorang ce inggris_
What's the area [dialling] code for …?	**Berapa nomor code wilayah untuk …?** _berrapa nomor code wilaya untuk_
I'd like a phone card, please.	**Tolong saya mau kartu telepon.** _tolong saya mow cartoo telepon_
What's the number for Information [Directory Enquiries]?	**Berapakah nomor telepon Penerangan?** _berrapaca nomor telepon pernerrangan_
I'd like the number for …	**Saya mau nomor telepon untuk …** _saya mow nomor telepon untuk_
I'd like to call collect [reverse the charges].	**Saya ingin collect call.** _saya ingin collect call_

On the phone   Telepon

Hello. This is …	**Hallo. Ini …** *halo. inee*
I'd like to speak to …	**Saya ingin bicara dengan …** *saya ingin bichara dengan*
Extension …	**Pesawat …** *persawat*
Speak louder, please.	**Tolong, bicara lebih keras.** *tolong bichara lebi ceras*
Speak more slowly, please.	**Tolong, bicara lebih pelan.** *tolong bichara lebi pelan*
Could you repeat that, please?	**Bisakah, anda ulangi lagi?** *bisaca anda ulangee lagee*
I'm afraid he/she's not in.	**Saya kira dia sedang tidak ada.** *saya cira dia serdang tidak ada*
You have the wrong number.	**Anda salah sambung.** *anda salah sambung*
Just a moment, please.	**Tolong, tunggu sebentar.** *tolong tunggoo serbentar*
When will he/she be back?	**Kapan dia kembali?** *capan dia cembalee*
Will you tell him/her that I called?	**Maukah anda beritahu dia bahwa saya menelepon?** *mowca anda beritahoo dia bawa saya telepon*
My name is …	**Nama saya …** *nama saya*
Would you ask him/her to call me?	**Maukan anda minta dia untuk menelepon saya.** *mowca anda minta dia untuk telepon saya*
I must go now.	**Saya harus pergi sekarang.** *saya harus pergee sercarang*
Thank you for calling.	**Terimakasih sudah menelepon.** *terrima kasi suda telepon*
I'll be in touch.	**Saya akan terus berhubungan.** *saya acan terus berhubungan*
Bye.	**Sampai jumpa.** *sampay jumpa*

Stores & Services

Indonesia is a great place for shopping, especially for arts and crafts. Prices are cheap and the range of items is enormous. Street vendors abound in tourist areas, but shopping off the beaten track is more relaxed.

ESSENTIAL

I'd like ...	**Saya mau ...** _saya mow_
Do you have ...?	**Apa anda punya ...?** _apa anda punya_
How much is that?	**Berapa harga itu?** _berrapa harga itoo_
Thank you.	**Terimakasih.** _terrima casi_

BUKA	open
TUTUP	closed
OBRAL	clearance [sale]

129

Stores and services
Pertokoan dan jasa

Where's ...? Dimana ...?

Where's the nearest ...?	**Dimana ... yang terdekat?** *dimana ... yang terdecat*
Is there a good ...?	**Apa ada ... yang bagus?** *apa ada ... yang bagus*
Where's the main shopping mall [centre]?	**Dimanakah pusat pertokoan yang besar?** *dimanaca pusat pertocoan yang bersar*
Is it far from here?	**Apa itu jauh dari sini?** *apa itoo jow daree sinee*
How do I get there?	**Bagaimana cara saya sampai ke sana?** *bagaimana chara saya sampay ce sana*

Stores Pertokoan

bakery	**toko roti** *toko rotee*
bank	**bank** *bank*
bookstore	**toko buku** *toco bucoo*
butcher	**tukang daging** *tucang daging*
camera store	**toko kamera** *toco camera*
cigarette kiosk	**kios rokok** *cios rocok*
clothing store [clothes shop]	**toko pakaian** *toco pacaian*
convenience store	**warung terdekat** *warung terdecat*
department store	**pusat pertokoan** *pusat pertocoan*
drugstore	**toko obat-obatan** *toco obat obatan*
fish store [fishmonger]	**tukang ikan** *tucang ican*
florist	**toko bunga** *toco bunga*
gift shop	**toko cenderamata** *toco chernderramata*
greengrocer	**toco sayuran** *toko sayuran*

health food store	**toko makanan kesehatan** _toco macanan cesehatan_
jeweler	**toko perhiasan** _toco perhiasan_
liquor store [off-licence]	**toko minuman keras** _toco minuman cerras_
newsstand [newsagent]	**kios koran** _cios coran_
pastry shop	**toko kue** _toco cue_
pharmacy [chemist]	**apotek** _apotek_
music store	**toko musik** _toco musik_
shoe store	**toko sepatu** _toco serpatoo_
souvenir store	**toko cenderamata** _toco cernderramata_
sporting goods store	**toko peralatan olahraga** _toco perralatan_
supermarket	**pasaraya** _pasaraya_
toy store	**toko mainan** _toco mainan_

Services Jasa

clinic	**klinik** _clinik_
dentist	**dokter gigi** _docter gigee_
doctor	**dokter umum** _docter umum_
dry cleaner	**toko penatu kimia** _toco penatu cimia_
hairdresser/barber	**salon/tukang pangkas rambut** _salon/tucang pangcas rambut_
hospital	**rumah sakit** _ruma sacit_
optician	**toko kacamata** _toco cachamata_
police station	**kantor polisi** _cantor polisee_
post office	**kantor pos** _cantor pos_
travel agency	**biro perjalanan** _biro perjalanan_

Hours Jam buka

City shopping malls [centres] and department stores are generally open from 8.30 am to 8 pm.

When does the … open/close?	**Kapan … buka/tutup?** *capan … buca/tutup*
Are you open in the evening?	**Apa anda buka sore hari?** *apa anda buca sore haree*
Where's the … ?	**Dimana …?** *dimana*
cashier [cash desk]	**kasir** *casir*
escalator	**tangga berjalan** *tanga berjalan*
elevator [lift]	**lift** *lif*
store directory [guide]	**Papan petunjuk pertokoan** *papan petunjuk pertocoan*
first floor [ground floor]	**lantai dasar** *lantay dasar*
second floor [first floor]	**lantai dua** *lantay dua*
Where's the … department?	**Dimana bagian …?** *dimana bagian*

SWALAYAN	self-service
OBRAL	clearance [sale]

LIFT	elevator [lift]
PINTU DARURAT	emergency exit
PINTU MASUK	entrance
TANGGA BERJALAN	escalator
PINTU KELUAR	exit
PINTU KEBAKARAN	fire exit
WAKTU	hours
TANGGA	stairs
KAMAR KECIL	restroom [toilet]

Services Pelayanan

Can you help me?	**Bisa anda bantu saya?**
	bisa anda bantoo saya
I'm looking for …	**Saya mencari …**
	saya merncharee
I'm just browsing.	**Saya hanya lihat-lihat.**
	saya hanya lihat lihat
It's my turn.	**Sekarang giliran saya.**
	sercarang giliran saya
Do you have any …?	**Apa anda ada …?** _apa anda ada_
I'd like to buy …	**Saya mau beli …** _saya mow berlee_
Could you show me …?	**Bisa anda memperlihatkan pada**
	saya …? _bisa anda mermperlihatcan_
	pada saya
How much is this/that?	**Berapa harga ini/itu?**
	berrapa harga inee/itoo
That's all, thanks.	**Itu saja, terima kasih.**
	itoo saja terrima casi

Selama pagi/siang bu/pak.	Good morning/afternoon, madam/sir.
Bisa saya bantu?	Can I help you?
Apa sudah semua?	Is that everything?
Ada lagi?	Anything else?

– Bisa saya bantu? (Can I help you?)
– Tidak terimakasih. Saya hanya lihat-lihat.
(No, thanks. I'm just browsing.)
– Baik. (Fine.) …
– Permisi. (Excuse me.)
– Ya, bisa saya bantu? (Yes, can I help you?)
– Berapa harga itu? (How much is that?)
– Hm, coba saya lihat … Harga seratus
tujuhpuluh rupiah.
(Hm, I'll just check … That's 170 thousand rupiah.)

Preferences Pilihan

I want something …	**Saya mau sesuatu yang …** _saya mow sersuatoo yang_
It must be …	**Harus yang …** _harus yang_
big/small	**besar/kecil** _bersar/cerchil_
cheap/expensive	**murah/mahal** _mura/mahal_
dark/light (color)	**gelap/terang** _gerlap/terrang_
light/heavy	**ringan/berat** _ringan/berrat_
oval/round/square	**lonjong/bundar/persegi** _lonjong/bundar/persegee_
genuine/imitation	**asli/imitasi** _aslee/imitasee_
I don't want anything too expensive.	**Saya tidak mau yang mahal.** _saya tidak mow yang mahal_
About … rupiah.	**Sekitar rupiah …** _sekitar rupiah_
Do you have anything …?	**Apa anda punya yang …?** _apa anda punya yang_
larger/smaller	**lebih besar/lebih kecil** _lebi bersar/lebi cerchil_
better quality	**lebih baik kualitas** _lebi baik cwualitas_
cheaper	**lebih murah** _lebi mura_
Can you show me …?	**Bisa anda memperlihatkan saya yang … ?** _bisa anda mermperlihatcan saya yang_
this/these	**ini/ini** _inee/inee_
that/those	**itu/itu** _itoo/itoo_

… apa yang anda mau?	What … would you like?
warna/bentuk	color/shape
kualitas/kuantitas	quality/quantity
Berapa banyak yang anda mau?	How many would you like?
Seperti apa yang anda mau?	What kind would you like?
Sekitar berapa harga yang anda bayangkan?	What price range are you thinking of?

COLOR ➤ 143

Conditions of purchase
Persyaratan pembelian

Is there a guarantee?

Apa ada garansi?
apa ada garansee

Are there any instructions
with it?

Apa ada buku petunjuk?
apa ada bucoo petunjuk

Out of stock Persediaan habis

Maaf, kami tidak punya.	I'm sorry, we don't have any.
Kami kehabisan persediaan.	We're out of stock.
Bisa saya memperlihatkan/ sesuatu yang lain?	Can I show you something else/ a different kind?
Mau kami pesankan untuk anda?	Shall we order it for you?

Can you order it for me?

Bisa anda pesankan untuk saya?
bisa anda pesancan untuk saya

Decisions Keputusan

That's not quite what
I want.

Bukan itu yang saya mau
bucan itoo yang saya mow

No, I don't like it.

Tidak. Saya tidak suka yang itu.
tidak. saya tidak suca yang itoo

– Selamat pagi. Saya mencari sweater.
(Good morning. I'm looking for a sweatshirt.)

– Baik. Warna apa yang anda mau?
(Certainly. What color would you like?)

– Tolong yang oranye. Dan saya mau
yang berukuran besar.
(Orange, please. And I want
something big.)

– Nah ini dia. Harga seratus tujuh puluh
lima ribu rupiah.
(Here you are. That's 175 thousand rupiah.)

– Hmm, itu bukan yang saya mau. Terima kasih.
(Hmm, that's not quite what I want. Thank you.)

Paying Membayar

Where do I pay?	**Dimana saya bayar?** *dimana saya bayar*
How much is that?	**Berapa harga itu?** *berrapa harga itoo*
Could you write it down?	**Bisa anda tuliskan?** *bisa anda tuliskan*
Do you accept traveler's checks [cheques]?	**Apa anda menerima cek pelawat?** *apa anda mernerrima chek pelawat*
I'll pay by …	**Saya akan bayar dengan …** *saya acan bayar dengan*
cash	**kontan** *contan*
credit card	**kartu kredit** *cartoo credit*
I don't have any small change.	**Saya tidak punya uang yang lebih kecil.** *saya tidak punya wang yang lebi cerchil*
Sorry, I don't have enough money.	**Maaf, uang saya tidak cukup.** *ma'af wang saya tidak chucup*
Could I have a receipt, please?	**Tolong bisa saya minta tanda terima?** *tolong bisa saya minta tanda terrima*
I think you've given me the wrong change.	**Saya rasa uang kembalian yang anda berikan pada saya salah.** *saya rasa wang cembalian yang anda berrican pada saya sala*

Dengan apa anda bayar?	How are you paying?
Transaksi ini tidak ditolak.	This transaction has not been approved/accepted.
Kartu ini tidak berlaku.	This card is not valid.
Boleh saya melihat kartu pengenal lain?	May I have additional identification?
Apa anda punya uang yang lebih kecil?	Have you got any smaller change?

Complaints Keluhan

This doesn't work.
Ini tidak jalan.
inee tidak jalan

Can you exchange this, please?
Bisa tolong tukarkan ini?
bisa tolong tucarcan inee

I'd like a refund.
Saya mau uang saya kembali.
saya mow wang saya cermbalee

Here's the receipt.
Ini tanda terima. *inee tanda terrima*

I don't have the receipt.
Saya tidak punya tanda terima.
saya tidak punya tanda terrima

I'd like to see the manager.
Saya mau ketemu manajer disini.
saya mow certermoo manajer disinee

Repairs/Cleaning Perbaikan/Pembersih

This is broken. Can you repair it?
Ini rusak. Bisa anda perbaiki?
inee rusak. bisa anda perbaiki

Do you have … for this?
Apa anda punya … untuk ini?
apa anda punya … untuk inee

a battery
baterai *baterray*

replacement parts
suku cadang *sukoo chadang*

There's something wrong with …
Ada yang salah dengan … ini.
ada yang sala dengan … inee

Can you … this?
Bisa anda … ini? *bisa anda … inee*

clean
bersih *bersi*

press
seterika *serterrica*

patch
menambal *mernambal*

Could you alter this?
Bisa anda permak ini?
bisa anda permak inee

When will it be ready?
Kapan ini selesai?
capan inee serlersay

This isn't mine.
Ini bukan punya saya.
inee bucan punya saya

The … is missing.
Ada … yang hilang.
ada … yang hilang

Bank/Currency exchange
Bank/Tempat penukaran uang

U.S. dollars are the most widely accepted foreign currency, but you can change all major currencies in main cities and tourist areas.

Where's the nearest …?	**Dimana … yang terdekat?** *dimana … yang terdecat*
bank	**bank** *bank*
currency exchange [bureau de change]	**tempat penukaran uang** *tempat pernucaran wang*

TEMPAT PENUKARAN UANG	currency exchange
BUKA/TUTP	open/closed
KASIR	cashiers

Changing money Menukar uang

Can I exchange foreign currency here?	**Bisa saya tukar uang asing disini?** *bisa saya tucar wang asing disinee*
I'd like to change some dollars/pounds into rupiah.	**Saya mau tukar dollar/pound ke rupiah.** *saya mow tucar dolar/ powned ce rupiah*
I want to cash some traveler's checks [cheques].	**Saya mau menguangkan cek pelawat.** *saya mow mengwangcan cek perlawat*
What's the exchange rate?	**Berapa nilai tukar?** *berrapa nilay tucar*
How much commission do you charge?	**Berapa komisi?** *berrapa comisee*
Could I have some small change, please?	**Bisa saya dapat uang kecil?** *bisa saya dapat wang cerchil*
I've lost my traveler's checks. These are the numbers.	**Saya kehilangan cek pelawat saya. Ini nomor.** *saya cerhilangan cek perlawat saya. inee nomor*

Security Beveiliging

Bisa saya melihat …?	Could I see …?
paspor anda	your passport
beberapa tanda pengenal	some identification
kartu bank anda	your bank card
Dimana alamat anda?	What's your address?
Dimana anda tinggal?	Where are you staying?
Tolong isi formulir ini.	Fill out this form, please.
Tolong tanda tangan disini.	Please sign here.

Can I withdraw money on my credit card here?

Bisa saya mendapat uang kontan dari kartu kredit saya disini?
bisa saya dapat wang kontan daree cartoo credit saya disinee

Where are the ATMs (cash machines)?

Dimana mesin ATM?
dimana mesin a te em

Can I use my … card in the ATM?

Bisa saya gunakan kartu … saya di mesin ATM ini? *bisa saya gunacan cartoo … saya dee mesin a te em inee*

The ATM has eaten my card.

Mesin ATM ini menelan kartu saya.
mesin a te em inee mernelan cartoo saya

MESIN ATM	automated teller (ATM)

The unit of currency in Indonesia is the rupiah (Rp.).

Coins: 25, 50, 100, 500, and 1000 Rp.

(The 25 Rp. coin has almost vanished.)

Notes: 500, 1000, 5000, 10,000, 20,000, and 50,000 Rp.

Pharmacy Apotek

Where's the nearest (all-night) pharmacy?	**Dimana apotek (24 jam) yang terdekat?** *dimana apotek (dua pulu empat jam) yang terdecat*
What time does the pharmacy open/close?	**Jam berapa apotek buka/tutup?** *jam berrapa apotek buca/tutup*
Can you make up this prescription for me?	**Bisa bikinkan resep ini?** *bisa bicincan rersep inee*
Shall I wait?	**Bisa saya tunggu?** *bisa saya tunggoo*
I'll come back for it.	**Saya akan kembali untuk ambil.** *saya acan cermbalee untuk ambil*

Dosage instructions Aturan pakai

How much should I take?	**Berapa banyak yang harus saya minum?** *berrapa banyak yang harus saya minum*
How many times a day should I take it?	**Berapa kali sehari harus saya minum?** *berrapa calee serharee harus saya minum*
Is it suitable for children?	**Apa ini bisa untuk anak-anak?** *apa inee bisa untuk anak anak*

Minum …	Take …
… tablet/… sendok teh	… tablets/… teaspoons
sebelum/sesudah makan	before/after meals
dengan air	with water
sekaligus	whole
pagi/malam	in the morning/at night
untuk … hari	for … days

DOCTOR ➤ 161

Asking advice   Mohon saran

I'd like some medicine for …	**Saya mau obat untuk …** *saya mow obat untuk*
a cold	**masuk angin** *masuc angin*
a cough	**batuk** *batuc*
diarrhea	**diare** *diare*
a hangover	**sakit kepala karena minum banyak** *sacit cerpala carena minum banyak*
hay fever	**alergi rumput** *alergee rumput*
insect bites	**gigitan serangga** *gigitan serrangga*
a sore throat	**sakit kerongkongan** *sacit cerrongcongan*
sunburn	**terbakar matahari** *terbacar mataharee*
motion [travel] sickness	**mabuk perjalanan** *mabuk perjalanan*
an upset stomach	**sakit perut** *sacit perrut*
Can I get it without a prescription?	**Bisa saya mendapatkannya tanpa resep?** *bisa saya merndapatcannya tanpa resep*
Can I have some …?	**Bisa saya minta …?** *bisa saya minta*
antiseptic cream	**krim antiseptik** *crim antiseptik*
aspirins	**aspirin** *aspirin*
condoms	**kondom** *condom*
cotton [cotton wool]	**kapas** *capas*
gauze [bandages]	**perban** *perban*
insect repellent	**obat nyamuk** *obat nyamuk*
painkillers	**penghilang rasa sakit** *pernghilan rasa sacit*
Band-Aid® [plasters]	**plester** *plester*
vitamins	**vitamin** *vitamin*

Toiletries Perlengkapan mandi

I'd like some …	**Saya mau …**	_saya mow_
aftershave	**calir cukur**	_chalir chucur_
deodorant	**pengawabau**	_perngawabow_
razor blades	**silet cukur**	_silet chucur_
sanitary napkins [towels]	**pembalut wanita**	_permbalut wanita_
soap	**sabun**	_sabun_
suntan lotion	**suntan lotion**	"suntan lotion"
factor …	**faktor**	_factor_
tampons	**tampon**	_tampon_
tissues	**tisu**	_tisoo_
toilet paper	**kertas toilet**	_certas toilet_
toothpaste	**pasta gigi**	_pasta gigee_

Haircare Perawatan rambut

comb	**sisir**	_sisir_
conditioner	**pembaik kondisi**	_permbaik condisee_
hair mousse/gel	**mousse rambut/jeli rambut**	_mus rambut/jelee rambut_
hair spray	**penyemprot rambut**	_pernyemprot rambut_
shampoo	**shampo/langir**	_shampo/langir_

For the baby Untuk bayi

baby food	**makanan bayi**	_macanan bayee_
baby wipes	**tisu basah untuk bayi**	_tisu basa untuk bayee_
diapers [nappies]	**popok sekali pakai**	_popok sercalee pakay_

Clothing Pakaian

General Umum

I'd like …	**Saya mau** _saya mow_
Do you have any …?	**Apa ada …?** _apa ada_

PAKAIAN WANITA	ladieswear
PAKAIAN PRIA	menswear
PAKAIAN ANAK	childrenswear

Color Warna

I'm looking for something in …	**Saya cari yang warnanya …** _saya charee yang warnanya_
beige	**abu-abu muda** _aboo aboo muda_
black	**hitam** _hitam_
blue	**biru** _biroo_
brown	**coklat** _choclat_
green	**hijau** _hijow_
gray	**abu-abu** _aboo aboo_
orange	**oranye** _oranye_
pink	**merah jambu** _mera jamboo_
purple	**ungu** _ungoo_
red	**merah** _mera_
white	**putih** _puti_
yellow	**kuning** _cuning_
light …	**… muda** _… muda_
dark …	**… tua** _… tua_
I want a darker/lighter shade.	**Saya mau warna yang lebih gelap/ lebih terang.** _saya mow warna yang lebi gerlap/lebi terrang_
Do you have the same in …?	**Apa ada yang sama warna …?** _apa ada yang sama warna_

Clothes and accessories
Pakaian dan aksesori

belt	**tali pinggang**	_talee pinggang_
bikini	**bikini**	_bicinee_
blouse	**blus**	_blus_
bra	**BH**	_be ha_
briefs	**celana dalam**	_chelana dalam_
coat	**jas**	_jas_
dress	**baju**	_bajoo_
handbag	**tas tangan**	_tas tangan_
hat	**topi**	_topee_
jacket	**jas**	_jas_
jeans	**jins**	_jins_
leggings	**pembalut kaki**	_permbalut cacee_
pants [trousers]	**celana panjang**	_chelana panjang_
pantyhose [tights]	**celana panti**	_chelana pantee_
raincoat	**jas hujan**	_jas hujan_
scarf	**syal**	_syal_
shirt	**kemeja**	_kermeja_
shorts	**celana pendek**	_chelana pendek_
skirt	**rok**	_rok_
socks	**kaus kaki**	_cows cacee_
suit	**pakaian formal**	_pacaian formal_
sweater	**sweter**	_sweter_
swimming trunks	**pakaian renang pria**	_pacaian rernang pria_
swimsuit	**pakaian renang wanita**	
	pacaian rernang wanita	
T-shirt	**kaus oblong**	_cows oblong_
tie	**dasi**	_dasee_
trousers	**celana panjang**	_chelana panjang_
underpants	**celana dalam**	_chelana dalam_
with long/short sleeves	**lengan panjang/pendek**	_lengan panjang/pendek_
with V-/round neck	**leher V/bundar**	_leher ve/bundar_

Shoes Sepatu

boots	**sepatu bot**	_serpatoo bot_
flip-flops	**sendal jepit**	_sendal jerpit_
running shoes [trainers]	**sepatu kets/latih**	_serpatoo cets/lati_
sandals	**sendal**	_sendal_
shoes	**sepatu**	_serpatoo_
slippers	**sepatu rumah**	_serpatoo ruma_

Walking/Hiking gear Perlengkapan jalan/naik gunung

knapsack	**ransel**	_ransel_
walking boots	**sepatu bot untuk jalan jauh**	_serpatoo bot untuk jalan jow_
waterproof jacket [anorak]	**jas kedap air**	_jas cerdap air_
windbreaker [cagoule]	**jas tangkal angin**	_jas tangcal angin_

Fabric Kain

I want something in …	**Saya mau yang bahannya …**	_saya mow yang bahannya_
cotton/denim	**katun/kain denim**	_catun/cain denim_
lace/leather	**renda/kulit**	_renda/culit_
linen	**kain linen**	_cain linen_
wool	**wol**	_wol_
Is this …?	**Apa ini …?**	_apa inee_
pure cotton	**katun asli**	_catun aslee_

HANYA BISA DI DRY CLEAN (PENATU KIMIA)	dry clean only
HANYA BISA DICUCI DENGAN TANGAN	handwash only
JANGAN DISETERIKA	do not iron
JANGAN DI DRY CLEAN	do not dry clean

Does it fit? Apa itu pas?

Can I try this on? **Bisa saya coba ini?**
bisa saya choba inee

Where's the
fitting room? **Dimana kamar pas?**
dimana camar pas

It fits well. I'll take it. **Ini pas sekali. Saya ambil ini.**
inee pas sercalee. saya ambil inee

It doesn't fit. **Ini tidak pas.** *inee tidak pas*

It's too … **Ini terlalu …** *inee terlaloo*

short/long **pendek/panjang** *pendek/panjang*

tight/loose **sempit/longgar** *sermpit/longgar*

Do you have this in size …? **Apa anda punya yang ini ukuran …?**
apa anda punya yang inee ucuran

What size is this? **Berapa ukuran ini?**
berrapa ucuran inee

Could you measure me, **Bisa tolong ukur saya?**
please? *bisa tolong ucur saya*

I don't know Indonesian **Saya tidak tahu ukuran Indonesia.**
sizes. *saya tidak tahoo ucuran indonesia*

Continental sizes are generally used throughout Indonesia.

Dresses/Suits						Women's shoes			
American	8	10	12	14	16	18	6	7	8	9
British	10	12	14	16	18	20	$4^{1/2}$	$5^{1/2}$	$6^{1/2}$	$7^{1/2}$
Continental	36	38	40	42	44	46	37	38	40	41

Shirts				Men's shoes								
American } British	15	16	17	18	5	6	7	8	$8^{1/2}$	9	$9^{1/2}$	10	11
Continental	38	41	43	45	38	39	41	42	43	43	44	44	45

1 centimeter (cm.) = 0.39 in.   1 inch = 2.54 cm.
1 meter (m.) = 39.37 in.   1 foot = 30.5 cm.
10 meters = 32.81 ft.   1 yard = 0.91 m.

Health and beauty
Kesehatan dan kecantikan

I'd like a … | **Saya mau …** *saya mow*

facial | **pembersihan muka** *permbersihan muca*

manicure | **manikur/rawat kuku** *manicur rawat cucu*

massage | **pijat** *pijat*

waxing | **pupur lilin** *pupur lilin*

Hairdresser Salon

I'd like to make an appointment for … | **Saya mau buat janji untuk …** *saya mow buat janjee untuk*

Can you make it a bit earlier/later? | **Bisa dibikin lebih awal/telat?** *bisa dibicin lebi awal/terlat*

I'd like a … | **Saya mau …** *saya mow*

cut and blow-dry | **potong dan blow** *potong dan blo*

shampoo and set | **shampo dan set** *shampo dan set*

trim | **potong sedikit** *potong serdicit*

I'd like my hair … | **Saya mau rambut saya …** *saya mow rambut saya*

highlighted | **diberi highlight** *diberee hailait*

permed | **dikeriting** *diceriting*

Don't cut it too short. | **Jangan gunting terlalu pendek.** *jangan gunting terlaloo pendek*

A little more off the … | **Dipotong sedikit lagi di …** *dipotong serdicit lagee dee*

back/front | **belakang/depan** *berlacang/derpan*

neck/sides/top | **leher/samping/atas** *leher/samping/atas*

That's fine, thanks. | **Sudah baik, terimakasih.** *suda baik, terrima casi*

Household articles
Peralatan rumah tangga

I'd like a(n)/ some ...	**Saya mau satu/beberapa ...** *saya mow satoo/berberrapa*
adapter	**adaptor/pemadan** *adaptor/permadan*
alumin[i]um foil	**kertas aluminium** *kertas aluminium*
bottle opener	**pembuka botol** *permbuca botol*
can [tin] opener	**pembuka kaleng** *permbuca caleng*
clothespins [pegs]	**jepitan jemuran** *jerpitan jermuran*
corkscrew	**pembuka botol anggur** *permbuca botol anggur*
matches	**korek api** *corek apee*
plug (electric)	**steker** *stecer*
plug (sink)	**penyumbat lubang tempat cuci** *pernyumbat lubang tempat chuchee*
scissors	**gunting** *gunting*
screwdriver	**obeng** *obeng*

Cleaning items Alat pembersih

dishcloth	**lap dapur** *lap dapur*
dishwashing [washing-up] liquid	**sabun cuci piring** *sabun chuchee piring*
garbage [refuse] bags	**plastik sampah** *plastik sampa*
detergent [washing powder]	**sabun cuci** *sabun chuchee*

Dishes/Utensils [Crockery/Cutlery]
Piring/Peralaran makan

bowls/plates	**mangkuk/piring** *mangcuk/piring*
cups/glasses	**cangkir/gelas** *changcir/gerlas*
forks/knives/spoons	**garpu/pisau/sendok** *garpoo/pisow/sendok*

Jeweler Toko perhiasan

Could I see …?	**Bisa saya lihat …?** _bisa saya lihat_
this/that	**ini/itu** _inee/itoo_
It's in the window.	**Yang di jendela etalase.** _yang dee jerndela etalase_
alarm clock	**weker** _wecer_
battery	**baterai** _baterray_
bracelet	**gelang** _gerlang_
brooch	**bros** _bros_
chain	**rantai** _rantay_
clock	**jam** _jam_
earrings	**anting-anting** _anting anting_
necklace	**kalung** _calung_
ring	**cincin** _chinchin_
watch	**jam tangan** _jam tangan_

Materials Bahan

Is this real silver/gold?	**Apa ini perak/emas asli?** _apa inee perrak/ermas aslee_
Is there a certificate for it?	**Apa ini ada surat?** _apa inee ada surat_
Do you have anything in …?	**Apa ada yang terbuat dari …** _apa ada yang terbuat daree_
copper	**tembaga** _termbaga_
crystal (quartz)	**kristal** _cristal_
cut glass	**gelas potong** _gerlas potong_
diamond	**berlian** _berlian_
gold (plate)	**emas (sepuhan)** _ermas (serpuhan)_
pearl	**mutiara** _mutiara_
platinum	**platina** _platina_
silver (plate)	**perak (lapisan)** _perak (lapisan)_

Newsstand Kios koran

Do you sell English-language books/newspapers?	**Apa anda jual buku/koran berbahasa inggris?** _apa anda jual bucoo/coran berbahasa inggris_
I'd like a(n)/some …	**Saya mau …** _saya mow_
book	**buku** _bucoo_
candy [sweets]	**permen** _permen_
chewing gum	**permen karet** _permen caret_
chocolate bar	**coklat** _choclat_
cigarettes (pack of)	**(satu bungkus) rokok** _(satoo bungcus) rocok_
cigars	**cerutu** _cherrutoo_
dictionary	**kamus** _camus_
English–Indonesian	**Inggris-Indonesia** _inggris indonesia_
envelopes	**amplop** _amplop_
guidebook of …	**buku panduan untuk …** _bucoo panduan untuk_
lighter	**pemantik api** _permantik apee_
magazine	**majalah** _majala_
map	**peta** _perta_
map of the town	**peta kota** _perta cota_
matches	**korek api** _corek apee_
newspaper	**koran** _coran_
American/English	**Amerika/Inggris** _america/inggris_
pen	**pulpen** _pulpen_
road map of …	**peta jalan untuk …** _perta jalan untuk_
stamps	**perangko** _perrangco_
tobacco	**tembakau** _termbacow_
writing paper	**kertas tulis** _certas tulis_

Photography Fotografi

I'm looking for a(n) ... camera.	**Saya cari kamera ...** *saya charee camera*
automatic	**otomatis** *otomatis*
compact	**kompak** *compac*
disposable	**sekali pakai** *sercalee pacay*
SLR	**SLR** *es el er*
I'd like a(n) ...	**saya mau satu ...** *saya mow satoo*
battery	**baterai** *baterray*
camera case	**tas kamera** *tas camera*
filter	**filter** *filter*
lens/lens cap	**lensa/penutup lensa** *lensa/pernutup lensa*

Film/Processing Film/Cuci-cetak

I'd like a ... film.	**Saya mau film ...** *saya mow film*
black and white	**hitam-putih** *hitam puti*
color	**berwarna** *berwarna*
24/36 exposures	**film isi dua puluhempat/tiga puluh enam** *film isee dua pulu ermpat/ tiga pul ernam*
I'd like this film developed, please.	**Tolong saya mau film ini di cuci-cetak.** *tolong saya mow film inee dee chuchee chetak*
Would you enlarge this, please?	**Bisa tolong memperbesar ini?** *bisa tolong merperbersar inee*
How much do ... exposures cost?	**Berapa harga film is ...?** *berrapa harga film*
When will the photos be ready?	**Kapan foto selesai?** *capan film serlersay*
I'd like to pick up my photos.	**Saya mau ambil foto.** *saya mow ambil foto*
Here's the receipt.	**Ini tanda terima.** *inee tanda terrima*

Post office Kantor pos

General queries Pertanyaan umum

Where's the post office?	**Dimana kantor pos?** *dimana cantor pos*
What time does the post office open/close?	**Jam berapa kantor pos buka/tutup?** *jam berrapa cantor pos buca/tutup*
Does it close for lunch?	**Apa tutup waktu makan siang?** *apa tutup wactoo macan siang*
Where's the mailbox [postbox]?	**Dimana kotak surat?** *dimana cotak pos*
Is there any mail for me?	**Apa ada surat untuk saya?** *apa ada surat untuk saya*

Buying stamps Membeli perangko

I'd like to send these postcards to …	**Saya mau kirim kartupos ke …** *saya mow cirim cartoopos inee*
A stamp for this postcard/letter, please.	**Tolong perangko untuk kartupos/surat ini …** *tolong perrangco untuk cartoopos/surat inee*
A stamp …, please.	**Tolong satu perangko …** *tolong satoo perrangco*
What's the postage for a letter to …?	**Berapa ongkos perangko untuk surat ke …?** *berrapa ongcos perrangco untuk surat ce*

– Halo, saya mau mengirim kartupos-kartupos
ini ke Amerika.
(Hello, I'd like to send these postcards
to the U.S.)

– *Berapa banyak?* (How many?)

– Sembilan. (Nine.)

– *Jadi dua ribu rupiah dikali sembilan:
delapan belas ribu rupiah.*
(That's two thousand rupiah times nine:
eighteen thousand rupiah, please.)

Sending packages Mengirim paket

I want to send this package [parcel] by …
Saya mau kirim paket ini lewat … _saya mow cirim pacet inee lewat_

airmail
udara _oodara_

special delivery [express]
ekspres _ecspres_

registered mail
surat tercatat _surat terchatat_

It contains …
Ini berisi … _inee berrisee_

Tolong isi laporan untuk pabean ini.	Please fill out the customs declaration.
Berapa nilai?	What's the value?
Apa isinya?	What's inside?

Telecommunications Telekomunikasi

I'd like a phone card, please.
Tolong, saya mau kartu telpon. _tolong, saya mow cartoo telepon_

10/20/50 units
sepuluh/dua puluh/limapuluh pulsa _serpulu/dua pulu/lima pulu pulsa_

I'd like to send a message …
Saya mau kirim … _saya mow cirim_

by e-mail/fax
e-mail/faks _eemel/facs_

What's your e-mail address?
Apa alamat e-mail anda? _apa alamat eemel anda_

Can I access the Internet here?
Bisa saya melihat internet disini? _bisa saya melihat internet disinee_

What are the charges per hour?
Berapa biaya per jam? _berrapa biaya per jam_

PAKET	packages [parcels]
PENGAMBILAN BERIKUT	next collection
PENGIRIMAN BIASA	general delivery [poste restante]
PERANGKO	stamps
TELEGRAM	telegrams

Souvenirs Suvenir

If you like arts and crafts, you'll have plenty of choice in Indonesia. Wood carvings are on sale everywhere. **Batik** and **ikat** (dyed woven cloth) are always popular. On Lombok and Java you will find good pottery. Bali is a shoppers paradise – you'll find everything there.

batik	**batik** _batik_
dolls	**boneka** _boneca_
lace	**renda** _renda_
leather puppet	**wayang kulit** _wayang culit_
pottery	**keramik** _cerramik_
wood carvings	**ukiran kayu** _oociran cayoo_
painting	**lukisan** _lucisan_
silverware	**barang-barang perak** _barang barang perak_
woven basket	**keranjang anyaman** _cerranjang anyaman_
antiques	**barang antik** _barang antik_

Gifts Hadiah

bottle of wine	**sebotol anggur** _serbotol anggur_
box of chocolates	**sekotak coklat** _sercotak choclat_
calendar	**kalender** _calender_
key ring	**gantungan kunci** _gantungan cunchee_
postcards	**kartu pos** _cartoo pos_
scarf	**syal** _syal_
souvenir guide	**buku petunjuk suvenir** _bucoo pertunjuk suvenir_
tea towel	**lap dapur** _lap dapur_
T-shirt	**kaus oblong** _cows oblong_

Music Musik

I'd like a …	**Saya mau …** _saya mow_
cassette	**kaset** _caset_
compact disc	**CD** _see dee_
record	**piringan hitam** _piringan hitam_
videocassette	**kaset video** _caset video_
Who are the popular native singers/bands?	**Siapa penyanyi/band dalam negeri yang terkenal?** _siapa pernyanyee/band dalam nergree tercenal_

Toys and games Mainan dan permainan

I'd like a toy/game …	**Saya mau mainan/permainan …** _saya mow mainan/permainan_
for a boy	**untuk anak laki-laki** _untuk lacee lacee_
for a 5-year-old girl	**untuk anak perempuan umur lima tahun** _untuk anak perrumpuan oomur lima tahun_
ball/chess set	**bola/catur** _bola/chatur_
doll/teddy bear	**boneka/beruang** _boneca/berruang_
electronic game	**mainan elektronik** _mainan electronik_
pail and shovel [bucket and spade]	**ember dan sekop** _ember dan scop_

Antiques antik

How old is this?	**Berapa umur ini?** _berrapa oomur inee_
Do you have anything from the … era?	**Apa anda punya barang jaman …?** _apa anda punya barang jaman_
Can you send it to me?	**Bisa anda kirimkan ke saya?** _bisa anda cirimcan ce saya_
Will I have problems with customs?	**Apa saya akan punya masalah dengan bea cukai?** _apa saya acan punya masala dengan bea chucay_

WHO?/WHAT?/WHEN? ➤ 103

Supermarket/Minimart
Pasaraya/Pasar mini

At the supermarket Di pasarraya

Excuse me. Where can I find …?

Permisi. Dimana bisa saya dapatkan …? *permisee. dimana saya dapatcan*

Do I pay for this here?

Apa saya bayar ini disini? *apa saya bayar inee disinee*

Where are the carts [trolleys]/baskets?

Dimana kereta [troli]/keranjang? *dimana kerreta [trolee]/cerranjang*

Is there a … here?

Apa disini ada …? *apa disinee ada*

pharmacy

apotek *apotek*

ROTI DAN KUE	bread and cakes
MAKANAN KALENG	canned foods
IKAN SEGAR	fresh fish
DAGING SEGAR	fresh meat
BAHAN-BAHAN SEGAR	fresh produce
MAKANAN BEKU	frozen foods
PERLENGKAPAN RUMAH TANGGA	household goods
AYAM	poultry

Weights and measures

- 1 kilogram or kilo (kg.) = 1000 grams (g.); 100 g. = 3.5 oz.; **1 kg.** = 2.2 lb. 1 oz. = **28.35 g.**; 1 lb. = **453.60 g.**

- 1 liter (l.) = 0.88 imp. quart or 1.06 U.S. quart; 1 imp. quart = **1.14 l.**; 1 U.S. quart = **0.951 l.**; 1 imp. gallon = **4.55 l.**; 1 U.S. gallon = **3.8 l.**

MAKAN DALAM WAKTU …	eat within … days
HARI SETELAH DIBUKA	of opening
SIMPAN DI LEMARI ES	keep refrigerated
DAPAT DIMASUKKAN KE MICROWAVE	microwaveable
COCOK UNTUK VEGETARIAN	suitable for vegetarians
MASA PAKAI SAMPAI …	use by …

At the minimart Di toko kecil

I'd like …	**Saya mau …** _saya mow_
this one/that one	**yang ini/yang itu** _yang inee/yang itoo_
these/those	**ini** _inee_
to the left/right	**di sebelah kiri/kanan** _dee serbela ciri/canan_
over there/here	**di sebelah sana/sini** _dee serbela sana/sinee_
Where is/are the …?	**Dimana …?** _dimana_
I'd like …	**Saya mau …** _saya mow_
a kilo (of)/half a kilo (of)	**satu kilo/setengah kilo** _satoo cilo/sertenga cilo_
a liter (of)/half a liter (of)	**satu liter/setengah liter** _satoo liter/sertenga liter_
… slices of ham	**… potong ham** _… potong ham_
apples	**apel** _apel_
bread	**roti** _rotee_
coffee	**kopi** _copee_
cheese	**keju** _cejoo_
eggs	**telur** _terlur_
jam	**selai** _serlay_
milk	**susu** _susoo_
That's all, thanks.	**Itu saja, terima kasih.** _inee saja terrima casi_

– Tolong, saya mau beli roti.
(I'd like some bread, please.)
– *Yang ini? (This one?)*
– Ya, yang itu. (Yes, that one.)
– *Baik. Itu saja? (Certainly. Is that all?)*
– Dan telor. (And some eggs.)
– *Nah, ini. (Here you are.)*

Provisions/Picnic Perbekalan/Piknik

beer	**bir** *bir*
bread	**roti** *rotee*
butter	**mentega** *merntega*
cakes	**kue basah** *cue basa*
cheese	**keju** *cejoo*
coffee	**kopi** *copee*
cooked meats	**daging masak** *daging masak*
cookies [biscuits]	**biskuit** *biscuit*
eggs	**telur** *terlur*
grapes	**anggur** *anggur*
instant coffee	**kopi instan** *copee instan*
jam	**selai** *serlay*
lemonade	**limun** *limun*
margarine	**margarin** *margarin*
milk	**susu** *susoo*
oranges	**jeruk** *jerruk*
rolls (bread)	**roti kadet** *rotee cadet*
sausage/salami	**sosis/salami** *sosis/salamee*
tea bags	**kantong teh** *cantong te*
wine	**anggur** *anggur*
yogurt	**yoghurt** *yogurt*

Police Polisi

Where's the nearest police station?	**Dimana kantor polisi terdekat?** *dimana cantor polisee*
Does anyone here speak English?	**Apa ada disini yang berbahasa Inggris?** *apa ada disinee yang berbahasa inggris*
I want to report a(n) …	**Saya mau laporkan sebuah …** *saya mow laporcan serbuah*
accident	**kecelakaan** *cechelaca'an*
attack	**penyergapan** *pernyergapan*
mugging	**penjambretan** *pernjambretan*
rape	**perkosaan** *percosa'an*
My child is missing.	**Anak saya hilang.** *anak saya hilang*
Here's a photo of him/her.	**Ini foto.** *inee foto*
I need an English-speaking lawyer.	**Saya perlu pengacara berbahasa Inggris.** *saya perloo pengachara berbahasa inggris*
I need to make a phone call.	**Saya perlu telpon.** *saya perloo telepon*
I need to contact the … Consulate.	**Saya perlu hubungi konsulat …** *saya perloo hubungee consulat*
American/British	**Amerika/Inggris** *america/inggris*

Bisa anda memberi gambaran mengenai dia?	Can you describe him/her?
pria/wanita	male/female
pirang/coklat	blond(e)/brunette
berambut merah/putih	red-headed/gray-haired
rambut panjang/pendek	long/short hair
botak	balding
perkiraan tinggi badan …	approximate height …
(perkiraan) umur …	approximate age …
Dia memakai …	He/She was wearing …

CLOTHES ➤ 144; COLOR ➤ 143

Lost property/Theft
Kehilangan barang/Kecurian

I want to report a theft.	**Saya mau laporkan sebuah pencurian.** *saya mow laporcan serbuah pernchurian*
My bag was snatched.	**Tas saya dirampas.** *tas saya dirampas*
My … has been stolen from my car.	**… saya dicuri dari dalam mobil saya.** *… saya dichuree dalam mobil saya*
I've been robbed/mugged.	**Saya dirampok/dijambret.** *saya dirampok/dijambret*
I've lost my …	**Saya kehilangan … saya.** *saya cehilangan … saya*
My … has been stolen.	**… saya dicuri.** *… saya dichuree*
camera	**kamera** *camera*
credit cards/money	**kartu kredit/uang** *cartoo credit/wang*
handbag	**tas tangan** *tas tangan*
passport	**paspor** *paspor*
purse/wallet	**tas/dompet** *tas/dompet*
ticket	**tiket** *tiket*
watch	**jam tangan** *jam tangan*
What shall I do?	**Apa yang harus saya lakukan?** *apa yang harus saya lacucan*

Apa yang hilang?	What's missing?
Kapan dicuri?	When was it stolen?
Kapan terjadi?	When did it happen?
Dimana anda tinggal?	Where are you staying?
Dari mana itu diambil?	Where was it taken from?
Dimana anda saat itu?	Where were you at the time?
Kami akan mencarikan penterjemah untuk anda.	We're getting an interpreter for you.
Kami akan memeriksa kasus ini.	We'll look into the matter.
Tolong isi formulir ini.	Please fill out this form.

Health

Indonesia is a tropical country with fairly low sanitation standards. It is quite easy to get ill. Make sure you have adequate travel insurance. It is recommended that you plan ahead and give yourself plenty of time for getting the necessary vaccinations. Discuss your requirements with your doctor. Carry proof of the vaccinations you have had with you.

Doctor (general) Dokter (umum)

Where can I find a hospital/ dental office [surgery]?	**Dimana ada rumah sakit/praktek dokter gigi?** *dimana ada ruma sakit/(practek) docter gigee*
Where's there a doctor/ dentist who speaks English?	**Dimana dokter/dokter gigi yang bisa berbahasa Inggris?** *dimana docter/docter gigee yang bisa berbahasa inggris*
What are the office [surgery] hours?	**Kapan jam buka praktek?** *capan jam buca practek*
Could the doctor come to see me here?	**Bisa dokter datang kesini?** *bisa docter datang disinee*
Can I make an appointment for …?	**Bisa saya buat janji untuk …?** *bisa saya buat janjee untuk*
today/tomorrow	**hari ini/besok** *haree inee/besok*
as soon as possible	**secepatnya** *sercerpatnya*
It's urgent.	**Ini sangat mendesak.** *inee sangat merndesak*
I have an appointment with Doctor …	**Saya ada janji dengan dokter …** *saya ada janjee dengan docter*

TIME ➤ 220; DATE ➤ 218

- Bisa saya ketemu dokter secepatnya?
  (Can I make an appointment for as soon
  as possible?)

- Kami penuh hari ini. Apa mendesak?
  (We're fully booked today. Is it urgent?)

- Ya. (Yes.)

- Baik, bagaimana kalau sekitar jam sepuluh
  lima belas dengan doktor Osman.
  (Well, how about at 10:15 with Doctor Osman.)

- Sepuluh lima belas. Terima kasih.
  (10:15. Thank you very much.)

Accident and injury Kecelakaan dan luka luka

My … is hurt/injured.	… saya sakit/luka. … _saya sacit/luca_
husband/wife	suami/isteri _suamee/isterree_
son/daughter	anak laki-laki/anak perempuan _anak lacee lacee/anak perrermpuan_
friend/child	teman/anak _terman/anak_
He/She is …	Dia … _dia_
unconscious	pingsan _pingsan_
(seriously) injured	luka (parah) _luca (para)_
bleeding (heavily)	berdarah (banyak) _berdara banyak_
I have a(n) …	Saya … _saya_
blister/boil	lecet/bisul _lechet/bisul_
bruise	luka memar _luca memar_
burn	luka bakar _luca bacar_
cut/graze	luka/goresan _luca/gorersan_
insect bite/sting	gigitan/sengatan serangga _gigitan/serngatan serrangga_
lump/swelling	benjolan/bengkak _bernjolan/bengco_
rash	gatal-gatal _gatal gatal_
sprained muscle	otot tegang _otot tergang_
My … hurts.	… saya sakit. … _saya sacit_

Symptoms Gejala

I've been feeling ill for … days.

Saya sudah tidak enak badan selama … hari.
saya suda tidak enak badan serlama … haree

I feel faint.

Saya pusing-pusing.
saya pusing pusing

I have a fever.

Saya demam. *saya dermam*

I've been vomiting.

Saya muntah-muntah.
saya munta munta

I have diarrhea.

Saya kena diare. *saya cena diare*

I have (a/an) …

Saya menderita … *saya merderrita*

cold/cramps

masuk angin/kram
masuk angin/cram

backache/earache/ headache/stomachache

sakit punggung/kuping/kepala/ perut *sacit punggang/cuping/ cerpala/perrut*

sore throat/sunstroke

sakit tenggorokan/kelengar matahari *sacit tenggorokan/ celengar mataharee*

Conditions Kondisi

I have asthma/arthritis.

Saya menderita asma/radang sendi. *saya merderrita asma/ radang sendi*

I'm …

Saya … *saya*

deaf/diabetic

tuli/diabetes *tulee/diabetes*

epileptic/handicapped

epilepsi/cacad *epilepsee/chachad*

(… months) pregnant

hamil … bulan *hamil … bulan*

I have a heart condition.

Saya punya masalah jantung.
saya punya masala jantung

I have high/low blood pressure.

Saya punya tekanan darah/rendah.
saya punya tecanan dara/renda

I had a heart attack … years ago.

Saya kena serangan jantung … tahun yang lalu. *saya cena serrangan jantung … tahun yang laloo*

Doctor's inquiries Pertanyaan doktor

Sudah berapa lama anda merasakan ini?	How long have you been feeling like this?
Apa baru pertama kali anda menderita ini?	Is this the first time you've had this?
Apa anda minum obat lain?	Are you taking any other medication?
Apa anda alergi sesuatu?	Are you allergic to anything?
Apa anda sudah disuntik vaksin anti tetanus?	Have you been vaccinated against tetanus?

Examination Pemeriksaan

Saya mau mengukur temperatur anda/tekanan darah.	I'll take your temperature/ blood pressure.
Tolong gulung lengan baju anda.	Roll up your sleeve, please.
Tolong buka baju bagian atas.	Please undress to the waist.
Tolong berbaring.	Please lie down.
Buka mulut anda.	Open your mouth.
Tarik napas yang dalam.	Breathe deeply.
Tolong batuk.	Cough, please.
Dimana yang sakit?	Where does it hurt?
Apa disebelah sini sakit?	Does it hurt here?

Diagnosis Hasil pemeriksaan

Anda harus di X-ray.	I want you to have an X-ray.
Saya perlu contoh darah/ feces/air kencing.	I want a specimen of your blood/stool/urine.
Anda harus ke dokter spesialis.	I want you to see a specialist.
Anda harus ke rumah sakit.	I want you to go to the hospital.
Ini patah/terkilir.	It's broken/sprained.
Ini tergeser/sobek.	It's dislocated/torn.

Anda menderita …	You have (a/an) …
usus buntu	appendicitis
kista	cystitis
flu	flu
keracunan makanan	food poisoning
patah tulang	fracture
radang lambung	gastritis
wasir	hemorrhoids
hernia	hernia
radang …	inflammation of …
campak	measles
radang paru-paru	pneumonia
sakit pinggang	sciatica
radang amandel	tonsilitis
tumor	tumor
penyakit kelamin	venereal disease
Ini kena infeksi./Ini menular.	It's infected./It's contagious.

Treatment Pengobatan

Saya akan member anda …	I'll give you a(n) …
obat antiseptik	antiseptic
obat penahan sakit	painkiller
Saya akan menulis resep …	I'm going to prescribe …
obat antibiotika	a course of antibiotics
Aapa anda alergi dengan suatu obat?	Are you allergic to any medication?
Minum satu pil …	Take one pill …
setiap … jam	every … hours
… kali sehari	… times a day
sebelum/sesudah makan	before/after each meal
bila terasa sakit	in case of pain
untuk … hari	for … days
Hubungi dokter kalau anda pulang.	Consult a doctor when you get home.

Parts of the body Bagian tubuh

appendix	**usus buntu**	_oosus buntoo_
arm	**lengan**	_lengan_
back	**punggung**	_punggung_
bladder	**kandung kemih**	_candung cemih_
bone	**tulang**	_tulang_
breast	**buah dada**	_bua dada_
chest	**dada**	_dada_
ear	**telinga**	_terlinga_
eye	**mata**	_mata_
face	**wajah**	_waja_
finger/thumb	**jari/ibu jari**	_jaree/ibu jaree_
foot	**kaki**	_cacee_
gland	**kelenjar**	_celenjar_
hand	**tangan**	_tangan_
head	**kepala**	_cerpala_
heart	**jantung**	_jantung_
jaw	**rahang**	_rahang_
joint	**sendi**	_sendee_
kidney	**ginjal**	_ginjal_
knee	**lutut**	_lutut_
leg	**kaki**	_cacee_
lip	**bibir**	_bibir_
liver	**hati**	_hatee_
mouth	**mulut**	_mulut_
muscle	**otot**	_otot_
neck	**leher**	_leher_
nose	**hidung**	_hidung_
rib	**tulang rusuk**	_tulang rusuk_
shoulder	**pundak**	_pundak_
skin	**kulit**	_culit_
stomach	**perut**	_perrut_
thigh	**paha**	_paha_
throat	**tenggorokan**	_ternggorocan_
toe	**jari kaki**	_jaree cacee_
tongue	**lidah**	_lida_
tonsils	**amandel**	_amandel_
vein	**pembuluh darah**	_permbulu dara_

Gynecologist Ahli kandungan

I have …	**Saya menderita …**
	saya mernderrita
abdominal pains	**sakit perut** _sacit perrut_
period pains	**sakit datang bulan**
	sacit datang bulan
a vaginal infection	**infeksi vagina** _infecsee vagina_
I haven't had my period for … months.	**Saya sudah tidak datang bulan selama … bulan.** _saya suda tidak datang bulan serlama … bulan_
I'm on the Pill.	**Saya minum pil anti hamil.**
	saya minum pil antee hamil

Hospital Rumah sakit

Please notify my family.	**Tolong beritahu keluarga saya.**
	tolong berritahoo celuarga saya
I'm in pain.	**Saya kesakitan.** _saya cesacitan_
I can't eat/sleep.	**Saya tidak bisa makan/tidur.**
	saya tidak bisa macan/tidur
When will the doctor come?	**Kapan dokter datang?**
	capan docter datang
Which section [ward] is … in?	**Dimana bagian …?**
	dimana bagian

Optician dokter mata

I'm near- [short-] sighted/far- [long-] sighted.	**Saya mata dekat/mata jauh.** _saya mata decat/mata jow_
I've lost …	**Saya kehilangan …**
	saya cehilangan
one of my contact lenses	**satu dari lensa kontak saya**
	satoo daree lensa contak saya
my glasses/a lens	**kacamata saya/satu kaca**
	cachamata saya/satoo cacha
Could you give me a replacement?	**Bisa anda menggantinya?**
	bisa anda mernggantinya

Dentist Dokter gigi

I have a toothache.	**Saya sakit gigi.**
	saya sacit gigee
This tooth hurts.	**Gigi yang ini sakit.**
	gigee yang inee sacit
I don't want it extracted.	**Saya tidak mau dicabut.**
	saya tidak mow dichabut
I've lost a filling/tooth.	**Tambalan gigi/gigi saya lepas.**
	tambalan gigee saya lerpas
Can you repair this denture?	**Bisa anda perbaiki gigi palsu ini?**
	bisa anda perbaici gigee palsoo inee

I'm going to give you an injection/an anesthetic.	**Saya akan memberi suntikan/ anastesi pada anda.**
You need a filling/cap.	**Anda perlu tambalan/crown.**
I'll have to take it out.	**Saya harus mencabutnya.**
I can only fix it temporarily.	**Saya hanya dapat memperbaikinya untuk sementara.**
Don't eat anything for … hours.	**Jangan makan apapun selama … jam.**

Payment and insurance
Pembayaran dan asuransi

How much do I owe you?	**Berapa saya harus bayar?**
	berrapa saya harus bayar
I have insurance.	**Saya ada asuransi.**
	saya ada asuransee
Can I have a receipt for my insurance?	**Bisa saya minta tanda terima untuk asuransi saya?** *bisa saya minta tanda terrima untuk asuransee saya*
Would you fill out this insurance form, please?	**Bisa tolong anda isi formulir asuransi ini?** *bisa tolong anda isee formulir asuransee inee*

Dictionary
English–Indonesian

Nouns and adjectives

There are, strictly speaking, no articles (a, an, the) in Indonesian, though **ini** (this) and **itu** (that) are sometimes used like articles for emphasis, e.g. **buku** (a book, the book), but also **buku ini** (this/the book), **buku itu** (that/the book).

Nouns may be made plural by duplication, e.g. **rumah** (house), **rumah-rumah** (houses). However, the singular form is usually sufficient to express plurality. The duplicated form is never used with such words as **banyak** (many) or **beberapa** (some): **banyak rumah**, (many houses), **beberapa piring** (some plates).

Pronouns

Indonesian pronouns do not show gender, for example **dia** means 'he', 'she,' or 'it'. There are two words for we, **kami** (excludes the person spoken to), **kita** (includes the person spoken to); **kami** is also sometimes used for 'I'. There are also infomal and formal pronouns, depending on the status and social position of those talking. This phrase book uses a neutral, polite form of 'you' – **anda**.

Here is a list of the most appropriate pronouns to learn first:

saya (kami) I	**anda** you	**dia** he, she, it
kami/kita we	**mereka** they	

Verbs

The basic form of a verb doesn't change in everyday speech, for example **saya bayar, anda bayar, kami bayar, mereka bayar** (I pay, you pay, s/he pays, we pay, they pay). In more formal speech and writing, prefixes and suffixes such as **mem-** and **-kan** may be added, though their use is not altogether standardized. So you may come across verb forms such as **membayar** (to pay), **memberikan** (to give).

Past tense

Sudah or **telah** may be placed before a verb to indicate the past, e.g. **Saya sudah makan** (I already ate). However, an adverb of time is generally enough, e.g. **Saya pergi kemarin** (I went yesterday).

Future tense

Akan before the verb indicates the future, but an adverb of time may be sufficient, e.g. **Saya akan bayar** (I will pay), but **Saya bayar nanti** (I'll pay later).

A-Z

A

a.m. pagi

about (*approx.*) kira-kira

abroad luar negeri

accept: to ~ (*authorize*) menerima; **do you ~ …?** anda menerima …?

accident (*road*) kecelakaan

accidentally tidak sengaja

accompany: to ~ menemani

accountant akuntan

acne jerawat

across seberang

acrylic akrilik

actor/actress aktor/aktris

address alamat

adjoining room kamar berdampingan

admission charge karcis masuk

adult (*noun*) dewasa

afraid: I'm ~ (*I'm sorry*) saya kira

after (*time*) setelah, sesudah

afternoon: in the ~ pada siang hari

age umur

ago: … years ago … tahun yang lalu

agree: I don't ~ saya tidak setuju

air: ~ conditioning AC; **~ mattress** matras tiup; **~ pump** pompa tiup; **~ sickness bag** kantung muntah; **~ mail** posudara

airport bandara

aisle seat kursi dekat gang

alarm clock weker

alcoholic (*drink*) alkohol

all semua

allergy alergi

allowance uang jalan

almost hampir

alone: leave me ~! jangan ganggu saya!

already sudah

also juga

alter: to ~ permak

alumin[i]um foil kertas aluminium

always selalu

am: I am saya

amazing menakjubkan

ambassador duta besar

ambulance ambulans

American (*adj.*) Amerika

American Plan (A.P.) termasuk makan pagi, siang dan malam

amount (*money*) jumlah

amusement arcade pusat hiburan

and dan

anesthetic anastesi

animal binatang

anorak jaket tahan air

another lain

antibiotics obat antibiotik

antique *(noun)* barang antik

antiseptic obat antiseptik; ~ **cream** krim antiseptik

any apa saja

anyone siapa saja; **does ~ speak English?** apakah ada yang berbahasa Inggris?

anything else? ada lagi?

apartment apartemen

apologize: I ~ saya minta maaf

appendicitis usus buntu

appendix usus buntu

appetite nafsu makan

apples apel

appointment: to make an ~ membuat janji

approximately kira-kira

April April

architect arsitek

are: are there ...? adakah?

area code kode wilayah

arm lengan

around sekeliling *(place)*; sekitar *(time)*

arrive: to ~ tiba

art gallery galeri seni

arthritis: to have ~ menderita radang sendi

artificial sweetener gula sintetis

ashtray asbak

ask: I asked for ... saya tadi pesan

asthma: to have ~ saya menderita asma

at: *(place)* di; *(time)* pada; **at last!** pada akhirnya; **at least** paling sedikit

athletics atletik

attack serangan

attractive menarik

audio-guide panduan audio

August Agustus

aunt tante

Australia Australia

authentic: is it ~? apakah ini otentik

authenticity keotentikan

automatic *(car)* otomatis; ~ **camera** kamera otomatis

automobile otomobil

autumn gugur

available *(free)* tersedia

avalanche tanah longsor

B **baby** bayi; ~ **food** makanan bayi; **~sitter** penjaga bayi; ~ **wipes** tisu basah untuk bayi

back: *(head)* belakang; *(body)* punggung; **I have a ~ache** saya sakit punggung

back: to be ~ *(return)* kembali

A-Z

bad buruk

bag tas

baggage: bagasi; **~ check** pemeriksaan; **~ claim** pengambilan bagasi

bakery toko roti

balcony balkon

ball bola

ballet balet

band *(musical group)* band

bandage perban

bank bank

barber tukang pangkas

basement lantai bawah tanah

basket keranjang

basketball bola basket

bath mandi; **~room** kamar mandi; **~ towel** handuk mandi

bathroom *(toilet)* kamar mandi

battery aki, baterai

battle site tempat peperangan

beach pantai

beam *(headlights)* lampu jauh

beard jambang

beautiful indah

because: karena; **~ of** karena

bed tempat tidur; **~room** kamar tidur; **~ and breakfast** tempat tidur dan makan pagi

bedding peralatan tidur

beer bir

before *(time)* sebelum

begin: to ~ memulai

beginner pemula

behind belakang

beige abu-abu muda

belong: this belongs to me ini milik saya

belt ban pinggang

berth tempat tidur

best terbaik

better lebih baik

between: *(time)* antara; **~ jobs** *(unemployed)* diantara pekerjaan

bib kain alas dada

bicycle sepeda

big besar; **bigger** lebih besar

bill *(restaurant, etc.)* tagihan

bin liner plastik keranjang sampah

binoculars teropong

bird burung

birthday hari ulang tahun

biscuits biskuit

bite *(insect)* gigitan

bitten: I've been ~ by a dog saya digigit anjing

bitter pahit

bizarre ajaib

black hitam; **~ coffee** kopi hitam; **~ and white film** *(camera)* film hitam putih

bladder kandung kemih

blanket selimut

bleach pemutih

bleeding: he's ~ dia berdarah

blind buta

blister lecet

blocked: to be ~ jadi tersumbat

blood darah; **~ group** golongan darah; **~ pressure** tekanan darah

blouse blus

blow-dry blow

blue biru

board: on ~ *(bus)* di dalam

boat trip pesiar dengan kapal

boil *(ailment)* mendidih

boiled *(cooking)* rebus

boiler mesin pemanas

bone tulang

book buku; **~store** toko buku

booted: to be ~ *(car)* diderek

boots boots

boring bosan

born: to be ~ lahir; **I was ~ in …** saya lahir di …

borrow: may I borrow your …? boleh saya pinjam … anda?

botanical garden kebun raya

bottle botol; **~ of wine** botol anggur; **~ opener** pembuka botol

bowel isi perut

bowls mangkuk

box kotak

boy laki-laki; **~friend** teman laki-laki

bra beha

bracelet gelang

brakes *(bicycle)* rem

bread roti

break: to ~ merusak

breakdown kerusakan; **~ truck** truk penderek

breakfast sarapan

breast buah dada

breathe: to ~ bernafas

bridge jembatan

briefs *(clothing)* celana dalam

bring: to ~ bawa

Britain Inggris

British Inggris

brochure brosur

broken: to be ~ jadi rusak; *(bone)* patah

bronchitis bronkitis

brooch bros

brother saudara

brown coklat

browse: to ~ *(look around)* me lihat-lihat

bruise luka memar

bucket ember

building bangunan

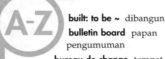

built: to be ~ dibangun

bulletin board papan pengumuman

bureau de change tempat penukaran uang

burger burger; **~ stand** penjual burger

burn luka bakar

bus bis; **~ route** rute bis; **~ station** stasiun bis; **~ stop** setopan bis

business: ~ class kelas bisnis; **to be in ~** terjun ke dunia bisnis; **on ~** dalam bisnis

busy: to be ~ *(occupied)* sibuk; *(full)* penuh

but tetapi

butane gas gas

butcher tukang daging

butter mentega n

button kancing

buy: to ~ beli; *(order)* pesan

by *(near)* dekat; *(time)* pada; **~ bus** dengan bus; **~ car** dengan mobil; **~ cash** dengan tunai; **~ credit card** dengan kartu kredit; **~ train** dengan kereta api

bye! sampai jumpa!

C **cabaret** kabaret

café kafe

cake kue

calendar kalender

call: to ~ for someone memanggil seseorang; *(telephone)* telepon; **call the police!** panggil polisi!

called: to be ~ dipanggil

camera kamera; **~ case** tas kamera; **~ store** toko kamera

camp: ~site tempat berkemah;

camp: to ~ berkemah

can: I can/I can't saya bisa/saya tidak bisa; **~ I have …?** saya minta …?

Canada Kanada

canal kanal

cancel: to ~ batalkan

cancer *(disease)* kanker

candy permen

can opener alat pembuka kaleng

cap *(clothing)* pelindung kepala; *(dental)* tambalan

car mobil; **by ~** dengan mobil; **~ park** tempat parkit mobil; **~ rental** sewa mobil; *(train compartment)* wagon

carafe karaf

caravan karavan

cards kartu

careful: be ~! hati-hati!

carpet *(rug)* karpet

carrier bag tas plastik

carry-cot tempat tidur lipat bayi

cart troli

case (*suitcase*) koper

cash (*money*) tunai; **~ desk** kasir; **~ machine** ATM

cash: to ~ (*exchange*) menukar uang

cashier kasir

casino kasino

cassette kaset

castle kastil

cathedral katedral

Catholic katolik

cave gua

cemetery kuburan

center of town pusat kota

ceramics keramik

certificate sertifikat

chain (*necklace*) rantai

change (*coins*) uang kembalian/uang kecil

change (*transportation*) ganti; (*money*) tukar uang; (*reservation*) rubah

changing facilities tempat mengganti popok

charcoal arang

charges biaya

charter flight pesawat carteran

cheap murah; **cheaper** lebih murah

check [cheque] book buku cek

charges biaya

check-in desk meja check in

cheers! terima kasih!

cheese keju

chemist apotik

chess catur

chest (*body*) dada

chewing gum permen karet

child anak; **~'s cot** tempat tidur bayi; **~minder** pengasuh anak: **~'s seat** kursi anak-anak; **children** anak-anak

Chinese (*cuisine*) masakan cina

chocolate coklat; **~ ice cream** es krim coklat

Christmas hari natal

church gereja

cigarette kiosk kios rokok

cigarettes rokok

cigars cerutu

cinema bioskop

claim check (*baggage*) tanda pengambilan

clamped: to be ~ diderek

clean bersih

clean: to ~ bersihkan

cliff jurang

clinic klinik

cloakroom tempat penitipan

clock jam

close (*near*) dekat

A-Z

close: to ~ *(store)* tutup

clothes pins [pegs] jepitan jemuran

clothing store toko pakaian

cloudy: to be ~ berawan

clubs *(golf)* clubs

coach bis; *(train compartment)* wagon; **~ station** stasiun bis

coast daerah pantai

cockroach kecoa

code *(area [dialing])* kode

coffee kopi

coin mata uang

cold dingin; **cold** *(flu)* pilek; *(weather)* dingin

cold: to have a ~ sakit pilek

collect: to ~ jemput, ambil

color warna; **~ film** film berwarna

comb sisir

come: to ~ datang; **to ~ back** *(return)* kembali

comfortable nyaman

commission komisi

company *(business)* perusahaan; *(companionship)* perkawanan

composer pencipta

computer komputer

concert konser; **~ hall** ruangan konser

concession konsesi

concussion: he has a ~ dia gegar otak

condom kondom

conductor dirigen

confirm: to ~ *(reservation)* astikan

congratulations! selamat!

connection *(train)* sambungan

conscious: he's ~ dia sadar

constant terus menerus

constipation susah buang air

consulate konsulat

consult: to ~ berkonsultasi

contact lens lensa kontak

contact: to ~ menghubungi

contagious: to be ~ menular

contain: to ~ berisi

contemporary dance tari kontemporer

contraceptive alat kontraseptif

cook: to ~ memasak; *(chef)* koki

cooker *(appliance)* kompor

cookies biskuit

cooking *(cuisine)* memasak; **~ facilities** fasilitas memasak

coolbox kotak pendingin

copper tembaga

copy salin

corkscrew pembuka minuman anggur

correct perbaiki

cosmetics kosmetik

cost: to ~ biaya

cotton katun; **~ wool** kapas mentah

cough batuk

cough: to ~ batuk

could: ~ I have …? bisa saya minta …?

country (nation) negara

courier kurir

course (meal) tahap; (track, path) tahapan; (medication) obat

cousin sepupu

cover charge karcis masuk

craft store toko kerajinan tangan

cramps kram

crèche penitipan anak

credit card kartu kredit; **~ number** nomor kartu kredit

crib tempat tidur bayi

crisps kerupuk

crockery sendok garpu

cross (crucifix) salib

cross: to ~ menyeberang

crowded ramai

cruise (noun) pesiar dengan kapal

crutches tongkat ketiak

crystal (quartz) kristal

cup cangkir

cupboard lemari

currency mata uang; **~ exchange** nilai tukar mata uang

curtains korden, tirai

customs bea cukai

cut (hair) gunting

cut glass kaca potongan

cutlery peralatan dapur

cycle route rute sepeda

cycling naik sepeda

cystitis kista

D

daily setiap hari

damage: to ~ merusak; **to be damaged** dirusak

damp lembab

dance: ~ tari (traditional)/dansa (modern); **to ~** menari, berdansa; **to go dancing** berdansa

dangerous bahaya

dark gelap; **darker** lebih gelap

daughter anak perempuan

dawn subuh

day hari; **~ ticket** tiket berlaku satu hari; **~ trip** perjalanan sehari

dead (battery) mati

deaf: to be ~ tuli

December Desember

deck chair kursi pantai

A-Z

declare: to ~ melapor
deduct: to ~ (money) mengurangi
deep dalam
defrost: to ~ mencairkan
degrees (temperature) derajat
delay tunda
delicious enak
deliver: to ~ mengantar
denim jins
dental floss benang pembersih gigi
dentist dokter gigi
denture gigi palsu
deodorant deodoran
depart: to ~ (train, bus) berangkat
department store pusat pertokoan
departure lounge ruang keberangkatan
deposit uang muka
describe: to ~ menggambarkan
dessert pencuci mulut
details perincian
detergent sabun cuci
develop: to ~ (photos) cuci, cetak
diabetic (noun) kencing manis; **to be ~** sakit kencing manis
dialling code kode panggil
diamond berlian
diapers popok
diarrhea: diare; **to have ~** kena diare

dice dadu
dictionary kamus
difficult susah
dining: ~ car gerbong makan; **~ room** ruang makan
dinner makan malam
direct (train, flight) langsung
direction: in the ~ of ke arah …
director (company) direktur
directory (telephone) petunjuk
dirty kotor
disabled (noun) cacad
discotheque diskotek
discount potongan
dish (meal) masakan
dishcloth lap piring
dishes sendok garpu
dishwashing liquid sabun pencuci piring
dislocated: to be ~ tergeser
display cabinet/case lemari kaca
disposable camera kamera sekali pakai
distilled water air yang disuling
disturb: don't ~ jangan ganggu
dive: to ~ menyelam
divorced: to be ~ bercerai
dizzy: I feel ~ saya pusing
do: to ~ melakukan
doctor dokter

doll boneka

dollar dolar

door pintu

double: ~ bed dua; **~ room** kamar untuk dua orang

downtown pusat kota

dozen lusin

draft [draught] draught

dress baju

drink (*noun*) minum; **drinking water** air minum

drip: the faucet [tap] drips keran bocor

driver supir; **driver's license** SIM

drive: to ~ mengemudi

drop: to ~ someone off mengantar seseorang

drowning: someone is ~ ada orang tenggelam

drugstore toko obat

drunk mabuk

dubbed: to be ~ di-isi suara

dummy (*pacifier*) dot

during sepanjang

dustbins tempat sampah

Dutch Belanda

E

e-mail e-mail; **~ address** alamat e-mail

ear telinga; **~ drops** obat tetes telinga; **I have an ~ache** saya sakit telinga; **~rings** anting-anting

earlier lebih awal

early awal

east timur

Easter Paskah

easy mudah

eat: to ~ akan

economy class kelas ekonomi

eggs telur

elastic (*adj.*) elastik

electric: ~ meter meteran listrik; **~ razor [shaver]** pencukur listrik; **electrical outlets** stop kontak

electronic elektronik; **~ flash** (*camera*) lampu kilat; **~ game** mainan elektronik

elevator lift

else: something ~ sesuatu yang lain

embassy kedutaan

emerald jamrud

emergency (*adj.*) darurat; **~ exit** pintu darurat

empty kosong

enamel email

end: to ~ mengakhiri; **at the ~** akhirnya

engaged: to be ~ bertunangan

engine mesin

engineering perekayasaan

England Inggris

English: Inggris; in ~ di Inggris;
~-speaking berbahasa Inggris

enjoy: to ~ menikmati

enlarge: to ~ *(photos)* perbesar

enough cukup

entertainment guide petunjuk hiburan

entrance fee karcis masuk

entry visa visa masuk

envelope amplop

epileptic: to be ~ menderita epilepsi

equipment *(sports)* peralatan

error kesalahan

escalator tangga berjalan

essential penting

evening malam

every setiap; **~ day** setiap hari;
~ hour setiap jam; **~ week** setiap minggu

examination *(medical)* pemeriksaan

example: for ~ sebagai contoh

except kecuali

excess baggage kelebihan bagasi

exchange rate nilai tukar

exchange: to ~ menukar

excursion perjalanan

excuse me *(apology)* permisi

excuse me: *(getting attention)* permisi; *(may I get past?)* numpang lewat; **excuse me?** *(please repeat)* maaf?

exhausted: I'm ~ saya lelah

exit *(noun)* keluar; *(highway)* jalan keluar

expensive mahal

experienced berpengalaman

expire: when does the card ~? kapan kartu habis berlaku?

exposure *(photos)* isi

express ekspres

extension pesawat

extra *(additional)* tambahan

extract: to ~ *(tooth)* mencabut gigi

eye mata

F fabric kain

face wajah

facilities sarana

factor *(sunscreen)* faktor

faint: to feel ~ oyong

fairground pekan raya

fall jatuh

family keluarga

famous terkenal

fan *(ventilation)* kipas angin

far: jauh; **~-sighted** pandangan jauh; **how ~ is it?** berapa jauh itu?

farm pertanian

fast cepat; **~-food restaurant** makanan cepat saji

father ayah

faucet keran

faulty: this is ~ ini rusak

favorite kesukaan

fax faks; **~ machine** mesin faks

February Februari

feed: to ~ beri makan

feeding bottle botol susu bayi

feel: to ~ ill merasa sakit

female perempuan

fever demam

few: sedikit

fiancé(e) tunangan

field lapangan

fifth kelima

fight *(brawl)* berkelahi

fill: to ~ out *(form)* mengisi; **to ~ up** *(with fuel)* mengisi penuh

filling *(dental)* tambalan

film *(movie)* film

filter saringan

find: to ~ mencari

fine *(well)* baik; *(penalty)* denda

finger jari

fire kebakaran; **~ alarm** tanda kebakaran; **~ department [brigade]** pasukan pemadam kebakaran; **~ escape** tangga darurat; **~ exit** pintu darurat; **~ extinguisher** pemadam kebakaran; **there's a ~!** kebakaran!; **~wood** layu bakar

first pertama; **~ floor** *(U.K.)* lantai pertama; **~ class** kelas satu

fish and poultry store toko ikan dan ayam

fish restaurant restoran ikan

fit: to ~ *(clothes)* mengepas

fitting room kamar pas

fix: to ~ perbaiki

flashlight lampu senter

flat *(puncture)* kempes

flavor: what flavors do you have? ada rasa apa saja?

flea lalat

flight penerbangan; **~ number** nomor penerbangan

flip-flops sandal

floor *(level)* lantai

florist toko bunga

flower bunga

flush: the toilet won't ~ kakusnya tidak menyiram

fly *(insect)* serangga

foggy: it is ~ cuaca berkabut

folk: ~ **art** rakyat; ~ **music** kesenian rakyat

follow: to ~ *(pursue)* mengikuti

food makanan; ~ **poisoning** keracunan makanan

foot kaki

football sepak bola

footpath jalan setapak

for *(time)* untuk; ~ **a day** untuk satu hari; ~ **a week** untuk satu minggu

foreign currency mata uang asing

forest hutan

forget: to ~ lupa

fork garpu

form formulir

formal dress pakaian resmi

fortnight dua minggu

fortunately untungnya

fountain air mancur

four empat; ~**-door car** mobil empat pintu

fourth ke empat

foyer *(hotel, theater)* lobi

fracture retak

frame *(glasses)* bingkai

free *(available)* kosong; *(no charge)* cuma-cuma gratis

frequent: how ~? berapa sering; **frequently** sering

fresh segar

Friday jum'at

fried goreng

friend teman

friendly mudah berteman

fries kentang goreng

frightened: to be ~ takut

from dari; where are you ~? anda berasal dari mana

front *(adj.)* depan; *(head)* wajah

frost beku

frying pan penggorengan

fuel *(gasoline [petrol])* bensin

full *(adj.)* penuh; ~ **board** termasuk makan pagi siang dan malam

fun: to have ~ bersenang-senang

furniture perabotan rumah

fuse sekering; ~ **box** kotak sekering

G **game** *(sport)* permainan; *(toy)* game

garage *(parking)* garasi; *(repair)* bengkel

garbage bags kantung sampah

garden halaman

gas (gasoline) bensin; ~ **station** pompa bensin; **I smell ~!** saya cium bau gas!

gastritis radang lambung

gate (airport) pintu

gauze perban

gay club klub homo

genuine asli

get: to ~ to ke; **to ~ back** (return) kembali; **to ~ off** (bus, etc.) turun; **how do I get to ...?** bagaimana cara ke ...; (buy) beli

gift hadiah

girl anak perempuan; ~**friend** pacar

give: to ~ beri

gland kelenjar

glass kaca

glasses (optical) kaca mata

glossy finish (photos) mengkilat

glove sarung tangan

go: to ~ (on foot) jalan; ~ **for a walk** jalan kaki; ~ **out for a meal** keluar makan; (by vehicle) pergi; ~ **shopping** pergi~ belanja; **where does this bus ~?** bus ini pergi kemana?; **let's ~!** ayo kita pergi!; ~ **away!** pergi!; ~ **on!** teruskan!

goggles kacamata renang

gold emas; ~ **plate** lapis emas

golf golf; ~ **course** lapangan golf

good selamat; ~ **afternoon** selamat siang; ~-**bye** sampai jumpa; ~ **evening** selamat malam; ~ **morning** selamat pagi; ~ **night** selamat malam; (delicious) enak

grandfather kakek

grandmother nenek

grapes anggur

grass rumput

gray abu-abu

great hebat

green hijau

greengrocer toko sayuran

grilled panggang

grocer (grocery store) toko bahan makanan

ground (earth) tanah; ~ **floor** lantai bawah

groundcloth [groundsheet] alas tanah

group kelompok

guarantee garansi

guide pemandu; ~**book** buku panduan; **guided tour** tur dengan pemandu; **guided walk** jalan kaki dengan pemandu

guitar gitar

gum permen karet

guy rope tali rami

gynecologist ginekolog

H **hair** rambut; **~dresser** salon; **to have a ~cut** potong rambut

half *(noun)* setengah; **~ past** setengah; **~ board** termasuk makan pagi dan makan malam

hammer martil

hand *(body)* tangan; **~bag** tas tangan; **~ washable** bisa dicuci pakai tangan

handicapped: to be ~ cacad

handicrafts kerajinan tangan

handkerchief sapu tangan

hanger gantungan

hangover *(noun)* sakit kepala setelah mabuk minuman

happen: to ~ terjadi

harbor pelabuhan

hard *(firm)* keras; *(difficult)* susah

hat topi

have: could I ~ …? bisakah saya dapat; **does the hotel ~ …?** apakah hotel ini punya; **I'll ~ …** saya mau …

hay fever alergi rumpat

head kepala; **I have a ~ache** saya sakit kepal

head waiter kepala pelayan

health: ~ food store toko makanan sehat; **~ insurance** asuransi kesehatan

hear: to ~ mendengar

hearing aid alat bantu dengar

heart hati; **~ attack** serangan jantung; *(cards)* hati

heat [heating] panas

heavy berat

height tinggi

help: can you ~ me? bisakah anda menolong saya

hemorrhoids wasir

her(s) punyanya; **it's hers** itu punyanya

here di sini

hi hai

high tinggi

highway jalan bebas hambatan

hiking *(noun)* mendaki; **~ gear** perseneling tanjakan

hill bukit

hire sewa

his punyanya; **it's his** ini punyanya

historic site tempat bersejarah

HIV-positive positif HIV

hobby *(pastime)* hobby

hold: to ~ on *(wait)* menunggu

hole *(in clothes)* lobang

holiday liburan; **on ~** dalam liburan; **~ resort** tempat berlibur

home rumah; **we're going ~** kami pulang ke rumah

homosexual (*adj.*) homoseksual

honeymoon: we're on our ~ kami dalam bulan madu kami

hopefully mudah-mudahan

horse kuda; **~ racing** kuda balap

hospital rumah sakit

hot panas; **~ spring** sumber air panas; **~ water** air panas

hotel hotel

hour jam; **in an ~** dalam satu jam

house rumah

housewife ibu rumah tangga

how berapa; **~ long?** berapa panjang?; **~ many times?** berapa kali?; **~ many?** berapa banyak?; **~ much?** berapa banyak?; **~ old?** berapa usia?; **~ are you?** apa kabarmu?; **~ are things?** bagaimana kabarnya?

hundred ratus

hungry: I'm ~ saya lapar

hurry: I'm in a ~ saya terburu-buru

hurt: to ~ luka; **to be ~** jadi sakit; **my ... hurts** ... saya sakit

husband suami

I **ice** es; **~ cream** es krim; **~ cream parlor** restoran es krim

icy beris

identification identifikasi

ill: I'm ~ saya sakit

illegal: is it ~? apakah itu tidak sah?

imitation imitasi

in (*place*) di; (*within period of time*) pada; **~ front of** di depan

include termasuk

included: to be ~ termasuk; **is ... included?** apakah ini termasuk?; **is this included in the price?** apakah ini termasuk dalam harga?

incredible luar biasa

indicate: to ~ menunjukkan

indigestion salah cerna

Indonesia Indonesia

Indonesian (*adj.*) Indonesia; (*language*) bahasa Indonesia

indoor pool kolam renang dalam ruangan

inexpensive tidak mahal

infected: to be ~ kena infeksi

infection infeksi

inflammation radang

informal (*dress*) tidak formal

information informasi; **~ desk** meja informasi; **~ office** kantor informasi

injection suntikan

injured: to be ~ terluka

innocent lugu

insect serangga; **~ bite** gigitan serangga; **to have an ~ bite** kena gigitan serangga; **~ repellent** obat nyamuk

inside di dalam

instant coffee kopi instan

instead of diganti

instructions instruksi

instructor instruktur

insurance (car) asuransi; (company) perusahaan asuransi; **~ card [certificate]** kartu asuransi

interest (hobby) kegemaran

interested: to be ~ in ... tertarik pada

interesting menarik

International Student Card Kartu Pelajar Internasional

interpreter penterjemah

intersection persimpangan

into ke dalam

introduce oneself: to ~ perkenalkan diri

invite: to ~ mengundang

iodine iodin

Ireland Irlandia

is: is it ...? apakah ...?; **is there ...?** apakah ada ..?; **it is ...** itu adalah ...

itch: it itches itu gatal

itemized bill bon yang terperinci

J

jacket jaket

jam selai

January Januari

jaw rahang

jeans jins

jellyfish ubur-ubur

jeweler toko perhiasan

job: what's your ~? apa pekerjaan kamu?

join: to ~ bergabung; **can we ~ you?** bisakah kami bergabung dengan kami?

joint sendi; **~ passport** paspor gabungan

joke lelucon

journalist wartawan

journey perjalanan

jug (water) kendi

July Juli

jumper cables kabel penyambung aki

jumper sweter

junction persimpangan jalan

June Juni

K

keep: to ~ menyimpan; **~ the change!** menyimpan saja kembaliannya!

kerosene minyak tanah; ~ **stove** kompor minyak tanah

ketchup kecap

kettle ceret

key kunci; ~ **ring** gantungan kunci

kiddie pool kolam renang anak-anak

kidney ginjal

kind *(pleasant)* baik

kind: what ~ of …? … jenis apa?

kiss: to ~ mencium

kitchen dapur

knapsack ransel

knee lutut

knickers celana dalam

knife pisau

know: to ~ mengetahui

L **lace** randa

ladder tangga

lake danau

lamp lampu

land: to ~ *(airplane)* mendarat

language course kursus bahasa

large besar; **larger** lebih besar

last *(in a row/sequence)* terakhir; *(year)* lalu

last: to ~ tahan

late lambat; **later** lebih lambat

laundry: ~ facilities fasilitas cuci baju; ~ **service** jasa cuci baju

lavatory kamar kecil

lawyer penasehat hukum

laxative obat cuci perut

lead: to ~ *(in a direction)* mengarahkan

leader *(group)* pemimpin

leak: to ~ *(roof, pipe)* bocor

learn: to ~ *(language)* belajar

leather kulit

leave: to ~ *(aircraft)* meninggalkan; *(on foot)* pergi; *(deposit)* meninggalkan; **I've left my bag** tas saya ketinggalan

left kiri; **on the ~** di sebelah kiri

left-luggage office tempat penitipan koper

leg kaki

legal: is it ~? apakah sah?

lemon jeruk nipis

lemonade limun

lend: could you ~ me …? bisakah saya pinjam … ?

length panjang

lens *(camera)* lensa; ~ **cap** tutup lensa

less kurang

lesson pelajaran

let me know! kasih tahu saya!

letter surat; **~ box** kotak surat

level *(adj.)* rata

library perpustakaan

license plate pelat nomor

lie down: to ~ berbaring

life: ~belt sabuk penyelamat; **~boat** kapal sekoci; **~guard** penjaga; **~jacket** pelampung

lift angkat

lift *(hitchhiking)* menumpang

light *(color)* terang, muda; *(weight)* ringan; **lighter** lebih ringan

light *(electric, bicycle)* lampu; **~ bulb** bola lampu

lighter *(cigarette)* pemantik api

like: to ~ *(people)* suka; *(want)* mau; **I don't ~ it** saya tidak suka itu; **I'd ~** saya mau

like this *(similar to)* seperti ini

limousine limusin

linen linen

line up antri

lip bibir

liqueur minuman keras

liquor store toko minuman keras

little *(small)* kecil; **a ~** sedikit

live: to ~ tinggal; **to ~ together** tinggal bersama

liver hati

living room ruang keluarga

local setempat

lock oneself out: to ~ terkunci diluar

lock kunci

lock: to ~ mengunci

long panjang; **~-distance bus** bis jarak jauh; **~-sighted** mata jauh

look: to ~ for mencari; **I'm looking for …** saya mencari …; **to ~ like** tampak seperti; **I'm just looking** saya hanya melihat

loose longgar

lorry truk

lose: to ~ hilang

lost: I've ~ … saya kehilangan; **to be ~** tersasar; **I'm ~** saya tersasar

lost-and-found [lost property] office kantor pengaduan barang hilang

lot: a ~ banyak

louder lebih keras

love: to ~ *(food)* suka; *(people)* cinta; **I ~ you** aku cinta padamu

lovely indah enak

low rendah; **lower** *(berth)* lebih rendah

low-fat rendah kalori

luck: good ~ selamat

luggage koper; **~ carts [trolleys]** kereta dorong

lump benjolan

lunch makan siang; **~ time** jam makan siang

lung paru-paru

M **machine washable** bisa di cuci di mesin cuci

madam nyonya

magazine majalah

magnificent bagus sekali

maid (hotel) pelayan; (home) pembantu

mail (noun) pos; **by ~** lewat pos; **~box** kotak pos

mail: to ~ menyurat

main utama; **~ street** jalan utama

make a phone call menelepon

make up: to ~ bikin

make-up dandan

male pria

mallet martil kayu

man laki-laki

manager manajer

manicure manikur

manual (car) buku pedoman

many banyak

map peta

March Maret

margarine margarín

market pasar

married: to be ~ menikah

mascara maskara

mask (diving) mask

mass massa

massage pijat

mat finish (photos) tidak mengkilat

match pertandingan

matches korek api

matter: it doesn't ~ masalah

mattress kasur

May Mei

may I bolehkah saya

maybe mungkin

meal makanan

mean: what does this ~? arti ini

measles campak

measure: to ~ mengukur

measurement ukuran

meat daging

mechanic montir

medication pengobatan

medicine obat

medium (position) tengah; (size) medium

meet: to ~ bertemu; **pleased to ~ you** senang bertemu anda

member anggota

men (toilets) pria

mention: don't ~ it tidak apa-apa

menu menu

message pesan

metal logam

midday tengah hari

midnight tengah malam

migraine pusing sebelah kepala

milk susu; **with ~** *(coffee)* dengan susu

million juta

mind: do you ~? apa anda keberatan?

mine saya punya; **it's ~!** itu saya punya!

mineral water air mineral

mini-bar minibar

minimart pasar swalayan kecil

minute menit

mirror cermin

missing: to be ~ kehilangan

mistake *(error)* salah

Modified American Plan [M.A.P.] termasuk makan pagi dan malam

moisturizer *(cream)* krim pelembab

monastery kuil

Monday Senin

money uang; **~ order** poswesel

month bulan

moped moped

more lebih; **~ slowly** lebih pelan; **I'd like some ~ …** tambah …

morning pagi hari; **in the ~** *(early morning/before noon)* pada pagi hari

mosque mesjid

mosquito bite gigitan nyamuk

mother ibu

motion sickness mabuk perjalanan

motor: ~bike Sepeda motor; **~boat** perahu motor; **~way** jalan bebas hambatan

mountain gunung; **~ bike** sepeda gunung; **~ pass** jalan pegunungan; **~ range** jajaran pegunungan

moustache kumis

mouth mulut; **~ ulcer** sariawan

move: to ~ *(motion)* bergerak; *(relocate)* pindah; **don't ~ him!** jangan gerakkan dia

movie film; **~ theater** bioskop

Mr. Tuan

Mrs. Nyonya

much banyak

mugged; I was ~ saya dijambret

mugging penjambretan

mugs cangkir

mumps gondok

muscle otot

museum museum

music musik
musician pemusik
must: I ~ saya harus
mustard mostar
my saya
myself: I'll do it ~ saya akan kerjakan sendiri

N **name** nama; my ~ is ... nama saya ...; **what's your ~?** siapa nama anda?

napkin lap
nappies popok
narrow sempit
national nasional
nationality kebangsaan
native dalam negeri
nature: ~ **reserve** cadangan alam; ~ **trail** lintas alam
nausea mual
near dekat; **nearest** terdekat; **~by** dekat dengan; **~-sighted** mata dekat
necessary perlu
neck *(head)* leher
necklace kalung
need: I ~ **to** ... saya perlu
nephew keponakan laki-laki
nerve saraf; **nervous system** sistem saraf

never tidak pernah; ~ **mind** tidak apa-apa
Netherlands Negeri Belanda
new baru
New Year Tahun Baru
New Zealand Selandia Baru
news: **~paper** koran; **~stand** [**~agent**] kios koran
next berikut; ~ **stop!** setapan berikut; ~ **to** di samping
nice menyenangkan
niece keponakan perempuan
night malam hari: **at** ~ pada malam hari; **for two nights** *(in hotel)* untuk dua malam; **~club** klub malam
no tidak; ~ **way!** tidak akan!
no one tidak satupun
noisy ribut
non-alcoholic tanpa alkohol
non-smoking bebas merokok
none tidak ada
nonsense! omong kosong!
noon siang hari
north utara
nose hidung
not bad tidak buruk
not yet belum
nothing tidak ada; ~ **else** tidak ada lagi

notify: to ~ beri tahu

November November

now sekarang

number nomor; **~ plate** pelat nomor; **sorry, wrong ~** maaf, salah sambung

nurse perawat

nylon nilon

O

o'clock: it's ... ~ sekarang jam ...

occasionally sekali sekali

occupied terisi

October Oktober

odds (*betting*) kemungkinan

of course tentu saja

off-licence toko minuman beralkohol

off-peak jam tidak sibuk

office kantor

often sering

oil minyak

old tua; **~ town** kota tua

olive oil minyak zaitun

omelet telur dadar

on: (*day*) pada; **~ foot** jalan kaki; **~ the left** di sebelah kiri; **~ the right** di sebelah kanan

on/off switch tombol hidup/mati

once sekali; **~ a day** sekali sehari

one like that satu seperti itu

one-way sekali jalan; **~ ticket** tiket sekali jalan

open terbuka; **~-air pool** kolam renang udara terbuka

open: to ~ buka

opening hours jam buka

opera opera; **~ house** gedung opera

operation (*medical*) operasi

opposite berlawanan

optician dokter mata, toko kaca mata

or atau

orange (*color*) oranye

oranges jeruk

orchestra orkes

order: to ~ memesan

organized hike/walk hiking berkelompok, jalan berkelompok

our(s) kami punya

outdoor di udara terbuka **~ pool** kolam renang udara terbuka

outrageous keterlaluan

outside di luar

oval lonjong

over: ~ here disebelah sini; **~ there** disebelah sana

overcharge: I've been overcharged saya membayar terlalu mahal

overdone terlalu lembek

overheat terlalu panas

overnight satu malam

owe: to ~ bayar; **how much do I ~?** berapa saya harus membayar kamu?

own: on my own sendirian; **I'm on my ~** saya sendirian

owner pemilik

P p.m. siang

pacifier dot

pack: to ~ mengepak

package paket

packed lunch makan siang dibawa dari rumah

paddling pool kolam renang anak-anak

padlock kunci gembok

pail ember

pain sakit; **to be in ~** kesakitan; **~killer** obat penghilang sakit

paint: to ~ mencat

painter tukang cat *(decorator)*, pelukis *(artist)*

painting lukisan

pair pasang; **a ~ of ...** satu pasang ...

palace istana

palpitations debaran

panorama pemandangan

pants *(trousers)* celana

panty hose celana stocking

paper napkins serbet kertas

paraffin lilin

paralysis lumpuh

parcel paket

parents orang tua

park taman

parking: ~ lot tempat parkir; **~ meter** mesin parkir

parliament building gedung parlemen

partner *(boyfriend/girlfriend)* pasangan

party *(social)* pesta

pass: to ~ *(a place)* melewati

passport paspor; **~ number** nomor paspor

pastry shop toko kue

patch: to ~ menambal

patient *(noun)* pasien

pavement trotoar; **on the ~** di trotoar

pay: to ~ bayar; **can I ~ in ...** bisa saya membayar dengan...; **~ phone** telepon umum

payment pembayaran

peak puncak

pearl mutiara

A-Z

pedestrian: ~ **crossing** penyeberangan jalan; ~ **zone [precinct]** daerah khusus pejalan kaki

pen pulpen

people orang

pepper merica

per: ~ **day** per hari; ~ **hour** per jam; ~ **night** per malam; ~ **week** per minggu

perhaps mungkin

period *(menstrual)* datang bulan; ~ **pains** sakit datang bulan

perm keriting

petrol bensin; ~ **station** pom bensin

pharmacy apotek

phone: to ~ menelepon

photo foto; **to take a** ~ berfoto; ~**copier** mesin fotokopi; ~**grapher** fotografer

phrase kalimat; ~ **book** buku ungkapan

pick up: to ~ menjemput

picnic piknik; ~ **area** tempat piknik

piece: a ~ **of …** sepotong …

pill pil; *(contraceptive)* pil anti hamil

pillow bantal; ~ **case** sarung bantal

pilot light lampu pilot

pink merah jambu

pipe *(smoking)* pipa

pitch *(for camping)* puncak

place: to ~ **a bet** bertaruh

plane kapal terbang

plans rencana

plant *(noun)* tanaman

plaster plester

plastic: ~ **bag** kantung plastik; ~ **wrap** bungkus plastik

plate piring

platform peron

platinum platina

play *(noun)* bermain; ~ **group** kelompok bermain; ~**ground** taman bermain; ~**ing field** lapangan bermain

play: to ~ bermain; **it is** ~**ing** *(movie, etc.)* sedang main

pleasant menyenangkan

please tolong

plug steker

pneumonia radang paru-paru

point: ~ **to** menunjuk

poison racun

Poland Polandia

police polisi; ~ **report** laporan polisi; ~ **station** kantor polisi

polyester poliester

pond kolam

popular terkenal

port *(harbor)* pelabuhan

porter portir

portion porsi

possible: as soon as ~ secepat mungkin

post *(noun)* pos; **~ office** kantor pos; **~age** perangko; **~card** kartu pos

post: to ~ mengepos

potato chips kentang goreng

potatoes kentang

pottery keramik

power: ~ failure mati listrik; **~ points** stop kontak

pregnant: to be ~ mengandung

prescribe: to ~ menulis resep

prescription resep

present *(gift)* hadiah

press: to ~ menyeterika

pretty cantik

price harga

priest pendeta

prison penjara

profession profesi

pronounce: to ~ mengucapkan

Protestant protestan

public *(noun)* masyarakat

pump *(gas station)* pompa bensin

puncture kempes; **have a ~** ban kempes

puppet show pertunjukan boneka

pure murni

purple ungu

purse tas

push-chair kereta dorong bayi

put: to ~ *(to place)* menaruh; **can you ~ me up for the night?** bisa saya menginap malam ini?; **where can I ~ …?** dimana bisa saya menaruh …?

Q **quality** *(adj)* kualitas

quarter: a ~ seperempat; **a ~ past …** jam … lebih seperempat; **a ~ to …** jam … kurang seperempat

queue: to ~ antri

quick/quickly cepat; **quickest: what's the ~ way?** bagaimana cara yang tercepat?

quiet tenang; **quieter** lebih tenang

R **rabbi** pendeta Yahudi

race course pacuan kuda

racetrack lapangan pacuan kuda

racket *(tennis, squash)* raket

railroad rel kereta

rain: to ~ hujan; **~coat** jas hujan

rape perkosa

rapids riam

rare *(steak)* mentah; *(unusual)* tidak biasa

rash alergi

razor pencukur; **~ blades** pisau cukur

ready: to be ~ siap

real *(genuine)* asli

rear belakang

receipt *(collection ticket)* tanda terima

receptionist resepsionis

reclaim tag tanda pengambilan

recommend: to ~ saran; **can you ~ …?** bisa anda sarankan … ?

red merah; **~ wine** anggur merah

reduction *(in price)* potongan

refreshments minuman/makanan ringan

refrigerator lemari es

refund: to give a ~ uang kembali

refuse bags kantung sampah

region *(geographical)* daerah; *(approximately)* **in the ~ of …** di sekitar daerah …

registered mail surat tercatat

register receipt tanda terima

registration form formulir pendaftaran

regular *(size)* sedang

reliable terpercaya

religion agama

remember: I don't ~ saya tidak ingat

rent: to ~ menyewa; **to ~ out** menyewakan

rental car mobil sewaan

repair: to ~ perbaiki

repairs *(car, etc.)* perbaikan

repeat: to ~ ulang; **please ~ that** mohon diulang

replacement *(adj.)* penggantian; **~ part** pengganti

report: to ~ *(crime)* melapor

require: to ~ permintaan

required: to be ~ *(necessary)* harus

reservation pemesanan; **~ desk** tempat (meja) pemesanan

reserve: to ~ esan; **I'd like to ~ …** saya mau memesan …

rest: to ~ istirahat

restaurant restoran

retired: to be ~ pensiun

return ticket *(train)* tiket pulang pergi

return: to ~ *(come back)* kembali; *(give back)* mengembalikan

revolting tidak enak

rheumatism rematik

rib tulang rusuk

rice beras *(uncooked)*/nasi *(boiled)*

right benar; **that's ~** itu benar; **on the ~** di sebelah kanan

ring cincin

rip-off (*adj.*) penipuan; **it's a ~** itu ~

river sungai

road jalan; **~ map** peta jala

robbed; I was ~ saya dirampok

robbery perampokan

rock music musik rock

rolls (*bread*) roti kadet

romantic romantis

roof (*house*) atap

room kamar

rope tali

round bundar; **~ neck** lingkar leher

round-trip (perjalanan) pulang pergi; **~ ticket** tiket pulang pergi

route rute

rubbish (*trash*) sampah

rucksack ransel

rude: to be ~ tidak sopan

ruins reruntuhan

run: ~ into (*crash*) menabrak; **~ out of** (*fuel*) kehabisan bensin

rush hour jam sibuk

S **safe** (*lock box*) kotak penitipan; (*not dangerous*) aman; **to feel ~** merasa aman

safety keamanan; **~ pins** peniti

sales (*as job*) penjualan; **~ tax** pajak ~; **~clerk** bagian penjualan

salt garam; **salty** bergaram

same sama

sand pasir

sandals sandal

sandy beach pantai berpasir

sanitary napkin [towel] pembalut wanita

satellite TV TV satelit

satisfied: I'm not ~ with this saya tidak puas dengan ini

Saturday Sabtu

sauce saus

sauna sauna

sausage sosis

say: how do you ~ …? bagaimana mengatakan …?

scarf selendang

scheduled flight penerbangan umum

sciatica sakit pinggang

scissors gunting

Scotland Skotlandia

screwdriver obeng

sea laut

seasick: I feel ~ saya mabuk laut

season ticket tiket musiman

seat (*on train, etc.*) kursi

second kedua; **~ class** kelas dua; **~ floor** lantai dua; **~-hand** bekas

secretary sekretaris

sedative obat penenang

see: to ~ melihat; *(inspect)* inspeksi; **~ you soon!** sampai jumpa!

self-employed: to be ~ wiraswasta

sell: to ~ menjual

send: to ~ mengirim

senior citizen orang tua

separately terpisah

September September

serious serius

service *(in restaurant)* pelayanan; *(religious)* kebaktian

serviette serbet

set menu menu paket

sex seks

shade warna, rindang

shallow dangkal

share berbagi

sharp tajam

shaving: ~ brush cukur; **~ cream** krem pencukur

she dia

sheath *(contraceptive)* kondom

sheet *(bed)* seperai

shirt *(men's)* kemeja

shock *(electric)* kejut

shoe: shoes sepatu; **~ repair** *(store)* toko reparasi sepatu; **~ store** toko sepatu

shopping: ~ area daerah perbelanjaan; **~ basket** keranjang perbelanjaan; **~ mall [centre]** pusat perbelanjaan; **~ cart [trolley]** troli; **to go ~** pergi perbelanjaan

short pendek; **~-sighted** mata dekat

shorts celana pendek

shoulder bahu

shovel sekop

show: to ~ tunjukkan; **can you ~ me?** bisa anda tunjukkan pada saya?

shower pancuran mandi; **~ room** kamar mandi

shut tutup

shut: to ~ tutup; **when do you ~?** jam berapa anda tutup?

shutter daun jendela

sick: I'm going to be ~ saya mau sakit

side: ~ order pesanan tambahan; **~ street** jalan kecil; **~ walk** trotoar

sides *(head)* samping, sisi

sights pemandangan

sightseeing: to go ~ melihat pemandangan; **~ tour** perjalanan melihat pemandangan

sign *(road sign)* tanda

signpost papan petunjuk

silk sutera

silver perak; **~ plate** lapisan perak

singer penyanyi

single: ~ room kamar untuk satu orang; **~ ticket** *(train)* karcis sekali jalan; **~ ticket** *(plane)* tiket pesawat; **to be ~** membujang

sink wastafel

sister kakak perempuan

sit: to ~ *(be seated)* **~ down, please** silakan duduk

size ukuran

skin kulit

skirt rok

sleep: to ~ tidur

sleeping: ~ bag kantung tidur; **~ car** gerbong tidur; **~ pill** pil tidur

sleeve lengan

slice: a ~ of ... sepotong ...

sliced meats daging potong

slippers sandal

slow pelan; **~ down!** perlambat!; **to be ~** lambat

slowly *(speak)* pelan-pelan

small kecil; **~ change** perubahan kecil; **smaller** lebih kecil

smell: there's a bad ~ ada bau yang tidak enak

smoke: to ~ merokok

smoking merokok

snack makanan kecil; **~ bar** cafe

sneakers sepatu kets

snorkel sonorkel

snow salju

soap sabun

soccer sepak bola

socket stop kontak

socks kaus kaki

soft drinks minuman ringan

sole *(shoes)* tapak

soloist pemain tunggal

soluble aspirin larutan aspirin

something sesuatu; **~ to eat** sesuatu untuk dimakan

sometimes kadang-kadang

son anak laki laki

soon segera

sore: it's ~ sakit; **~ throat** sakit kerongkongan; **I have a ~ throat** saya sakit kerongkongan

sorry! maaf

soul music musik soul

sour asam

south selatan

South Africa Afrika Selatan

South African *(noun)* orang Afrika Selatan

souvenir suvenir, cenderamata; **~ store** toko suvenir

space tempat

spade sekop

spare *(replacement)* pengganti; *(extra)* cadangan

speak: to ~ berbicara; **do you ~ English?** anda berbahasa Inggris?; **~ to someone** berbicara kepada sesorang

special khusus; **~ delivery** titipan kilat

specialist spesialis

specimen contoh

spectacles kacamata

spell: to ~ mengeja

spend: to ~ *(time/money)* menghabiskan

spicy pedas

sponge sepon

spoon sendok

sport olahraga

sporting goods store toko peralatan olah raga

sports: ~ club klub olahraga; **~ ground** lapangan olahraga

spot *(place, site)* tempat

sprained: to be ~ terkilir

spring musim semi

square lapangan, persegi empat

stadium stadion

staff pegawai

stain noda; **~less steel** baja anti karat

stairs tangga

stamp perangko

stand: to ~ in line antri

start: to ~ *(car, etc.)* nyala mulai

statement *(police)* pernyataan

stationer's alat tulis menulis

statue patung

stay: to ~ *(remain)* tinggal

steal: to ~ mencuri

stiff neck leher kaku

still: I'm ~ waiting saya masih menunggu

stolen *(adj.)* curian

stomach perut; **I have a ~ache** saya sakit perut

stool *(faeces)* tinja

stop *(bus/tram/etc.)* setopan

stop: to ~ *(train)* berhenti; **to ~ at** berhenti di

store guide petunjuk pertokoan

stormy berangin keras

stove kompor

straight ahead terus

strained *(muscle)* keseleo

strange aneh

straw sedotan

strawberry stroberi

stream sungai kecil

streetcar mobil

stroller kereta dorong bayi

strong kuat

student pelajar, mahasiswa

study: to ~ belajar

style gaya

subtitled: to be ~ dengan

sugar gula

suggest: to ~ menyarankan

suit sesuai

suitable bisa; **~ for** bisa untuk

summer musim panas

sun matahari; **to ~bathe** mandi matahari; **~glasses** kaca mata hitam; **~shade** payung; **~stroke** kelengar matahari; **sunny** terik

Sunday Minggu

super *(gas)* premix

superb luar biasa

supermarket pasar swalayan

supervision pengawasan

supplement tambahan

suppositories suppositori

sure: are you ~? anda yakin?

surname nama keluarga

sweater sweter

sweet *(taste)* manis

sweets permen

swelling bengkak

swim: to ~ renang; **~suit** pakaian renang

swimming berenang; **~ pool** kolam berenang; **~ trunks** celana berenang

swollen: to be ~ bengkak

symptom *(illness)* gejala

synagogue sinagog

synthetic sintetis

 T-shirt kaus oblong

table meja

take: to ~ *(medicine)* minum; *(time)* makan waktu; *(carry)* mengambil; **to ~ away** bawa; **to ~ out** *(extract tooth)* mencabut; **to ~ photographs** mengambil foto; **I'll ~ it** *(room)* saya ambil; **is this seat taken?** apakah kursi ini ada yang punya?; **~ me to ...** antar saya ke ...

talk: to ~ berbicara

tall tinggi

tampons tampon

tan *(skin color)* coklat

tap keran

taxi taksi; **~ stand [rank]** antrian taksi

tea teh; **~ bags** kantung teh; **~ towel** lap dapur; **~spoons** sendok teh

teacher guru

team tim

teddy bear tedi beruang

telephone telepon; **to ~** menelepon; **~ bill** tagihan telepon; **~ booth** tempat telepon; **~ number** nomor telepon

A-Z

tell: to ~ menjelaskan; **can you ~ me ...?** bisakah anda menjelaskan kepada saya?

temperature *(body)* suhu

temple pura, candi, kuil

temporarily sementara

tennis tenis; **~ court** lapangan tenis

tent tenda; **~ pegs** pasak tenda; **~ pole** tiang tenda

terrace teras

terrible buruk

terrific luar biasa

tetanus tetanus

thank you terima kasih

that itu; **~ one** yang itu; **~'s true!** itu benar; **~'s all** itu saja

theater teater

theft pencurian

their(s) punya mereka

then *(time)* dulu

there disana; **~ is/are ...** ada ...; **over ~** disana

thermometer termometer

thermos bottle termos

these ini

they mereka

thick tebal

thief pencuri

thigh paha

thin *(opp. thick)* tipis; *(narrow)* sempit; *(opp. fat)* kurus

think: I ~ saya pikir; **to ~ about something** memikirkan sesuatu

third ketiga; **a ~** sepertiga; **~ party insurance** asuransi pihak ketiga

thirsty: I am ~ saya haus

this ini; **~ one** yang ini

those itu

thousand ribu

throat kerongkongan

thrombosis trombosa

through melalui

thumb jempol

Thursday Kamis

ticket *(train)* tiket, karcis; **~ office** penjualan tiket

tie dasi

tight ketat

tights celana panjang ketat

till receipt tanda terima

time waktu; **is it on ~?** *(train, etc.)* apakah tepat waktu?; **free ~** waktu bebas; **what's the ~?** jam berapa?; **~table** jadwal

tin opener pembuka kaleng

tire ban

tired: I'm ~ saya lelah

tissue tisu

to *(place)* ke

tobacco tembakau

tobacconist penjual tembakau

today hari ini

toe jari kaki

toilet toilet, WC, tandas; **~ paper** kertas WC

tomatoes tomat

tomorrow besok

tongue lidah

tonight malam ini

tonsilitis radang amandel

tonsils amandel

too *(extreme)* terlalu; **~ much** terlalu banyak

tooth gigi; **~brush** sikat gigi; **~paste** pasta gigi; **I have a ~ache** saya sakit gigi

top *(head)* atas

torch sentelop

torn: to be ~ *(muscle)* jadi sobek; **this is ~** ini sobek

tough *(food)* keras

tour perjalanan; **~ guide** pemandu wisata; **~ operator** agen perjalanan

tourist turis, wisatawan; **~ office** pusat informasi wisata

tow truck truk penggeret

towel handuk

tower menara

town kota; **~ hall** balai kota

toy mainan

traditional tradisional

traffic lalu lintas; **~ jam** kemacetan lalu lintas; **~light** lampu lalu lintas; **~ violation** [offence] pelanggaran lalu lintas

trailer gandengan

train kereta api; **~ station** stasiun kereta api

trained terlatih

tram trem

translate: to ~ menterjemahkan

translation terjemahan

translator penterjemah

trashcans tempat sampah

travel: ~ agency agen perjalanan; **~ sickness** mabuk perjalanan

tray baki

tree pohon

trip perjalanan

trolley troli

trousers celana panjang; **trouser press** penekan celana panjang

truck truk

true: that's not ~ itu tidak benar

try: ~ on *(clothes)* mencoba

Tuesday Selasa

tumor tumor

tunnel terowongan

A-Z

turn: to ~ down *(volume, heat)* mengecilkan; to ~ off mematikan; to ~ on menghidupkan; to ~ up *(volume)* membesarkan

TV televisi

tweezers jepitan

twice dua kali; ~ a day dua kali sehari

twin beds dua tempat tidur

twist: I've twisted my ankle pergelangan kaki saya keseleo

two-door car mobil dua pintu

type jenis; what ~ of ...? ... jenis apa?

typical khas

tyre ban

U

U.K. Inggris

U.S. Amerika Serikat

ugly jelek

ulcer bisul

umbrella payung

uncle paman

unconscious: to be ~ jadi pingsan; he's ~ dia jadi pingsan

under di bawah

underdone *(not cooked/rare meat)* kurang masak

underpants celana dalam

understand: to ~ mengerti; do you ~? anda mengerti ?; I don't ~ saya tidak mengerti

undress: to ~ buka baju

uneven *(ground)* tidak rata

unfortunately sayangnya

uniform seragam

unit *(for a phone card)* pulsa

unleaded gas [petrol] bahan bakar unleaded

unlimited mileage tanpa batasan kilometer

unlock: to ~ buka kunci

unpleasant tidak menyenangkan

unscrew: to ~ melepaskan

until sampai

up to sampai

upper *(berth)* di atas

upset stomach sakit perut

urine air kencing

use: to ~ menggunakan; for my personal ~ untuk keperluan pribadi saya

utensils *(knives, etc.)* peralatan dapur

V

V-neck leher-V

vacant kosong

vacation liburan; on ~ berlibur

vaccinated against: to be ~ disuntik vaksin

vaginal infection infeksi vagina

valid berlaku

validate: to ~ *(tickets)* disahkan

valley lembah

valuable berharga

valve katup

vanilla *(flavor)* vanila

VAT PPN; **~ receipt** tanda terima PPN

vegetables sayur-sayuran

vegetarian vegetarian

vein urat

venereal disease penyakit kelamin

ventilator kipas angin

very sangat; **~ good** sangat baik

video video; **~ recorder** mesin video; **~cassette** kaset video

viewpoint tempat melihat pemandangan

village kampung

vinegar cuka

vineyard kebun anggur

visa visa

visit: to ~ berkunjung; *(hospital)* **visiting hours** jam berkunjung, jam besuk

vitamin pill tablet vitamin

volleyball bola volley

voltage voltase

vomit: to ~ muntah

W **wait: to ~** tunggu; **to ~ for** menunggu

waiter/waitress pelayan

waiting room ruang tunggu

wake bangun; **to ~ someone** membangunkan seseorang; **~-up call** telepon bangun pagi

walk home: to ~ jalan pulang

walking: ~ boots sepatu bot untuk jalan jauh; **~ route** rute perjalanan

wallet dompet

war memorial tugu pahlawan

ward *(hospital)* ruang

warm hangat; **warmer** penghangat

washbasin wastafel

washing: ~ machine mesin cuci; **~ powder** sabun deterjen; **~-up liquid** sabun cuci piring cair

wasp tawon

watch arloji

water air; **~ bottle** botol air; **~ heater** pemanas air; **~ skis** ski air; **~ fall** air terjun; **~ proof** tahan air; **~proof jacket** jaket tahan air

wave gelombang

way: I've lost my ~ saya tersasar

we kami; **we'd like ...** ... kami mau

wear: to ~ akai

weather cuaca; **~ forecast** ramalan cuaca

wedding perkawinan; **~ ring** cincin perkawinan

Wednesday Rabu

week minggu

weekend akhir pekan; **~ rate** [tarif] tarif akhir pekan

weight: my ~ is ... berat saya ...

welcome to ... selamat datang di ...

well-done (steak) matang

west barat

wet basah

what? apa?; **~ kind is it?** jenis apa itu?; **~ time?** jam berapa?

wheelchair kursi roda

when? kapan?

where? dimana?; **~ is?** dimana?; **~ were you born?** dimana anda lahir?

which? yang mana?

white putih; **~ wine** anggur putih

who? siapa?

whose? siapa?

why? kenapa?; **~ not?** kenapa tidak?

wide luas

wife istri

wildlife margasatwa

wind: ~breaker penahan angin

window jendela; (store) etalase; **~ seat** kursi dekat jendela

windy: to be ~ berangin

wine minuman anggur; **~ cellar** gudang minuman anggur; **~ list** daftar minuman anggur; **winery** perkebunan anggur

winter musim dingin

wishes: best ~ salam

with dengan

withdraw: to ~ mengambil uang kas

within (time) dalam waktu

without tanpa

witness saksi

wood kayu

wool wol

work: to ~ (function) bekerja

work: it doesn't work tidak bekerja

worse lebih buruk; **worst** terburuk

write down: to ~ menulis

writing paper kertas tulis

wrong salah; **~ number** (telephone) salah sambung; **there's something ~ with ...** ada yang salah dengan ...

x-ray sinar-x

year tahun

yellow kuning

yes ya

yesterday kemarin

yogurt yogurt

you *(formal)* anda; *(informal)* kamu

young muda

your(s) *(formal)* punya anda;
  (informal) punyamu

youth hostel wisma pemuda

zebra crossing penyeberangan
  jalan

zero nol

zip(per) ritsleting

zoo kebun binatang

Glossary
Indonesian–English

The Indonesian-English glossary covers all the areas where you may need to decode written Indonesian: hotels, public buildings, restaurants, stores, ticket offices, airports, and stations. The Indonesian is written in large type to help you identify the character(s) from the signs you see around you.

General

KIRI	_ci_ree	LEFT
KANAN	_ca_nan	RIGHT
MASUK	_ma_suk	ENTRANCE
KELUAR	cerlu_ar_	EXIT
KAMAR KECIL	_ca_mar cer_chil_	TOILETS
PRIA	_pria_	MEN (TOILETS)
WANITA	wan_i_ta	WOMEN (TOILETS)
DIPAKAI	di_pa_cay	OCCUPIED
TARIK/DORONG	_ta_rik/_do_rong	PULL/PUSH
DILARANG MEROKOK	di_la_rang mer_ro_cock	NO SMOKING
BAHAYA	ba_ha_ya	DANGER
DILARANG MASUK	di_la_rang _ma_suk	NO ENTRY

General

BARANG HILANG	_barang hilang_	LOST PROPERTY
DILARANG BERENANG	_dilarang berrenang_	NO SWIMMING
AIR MINUM	_air minum_	DRINKING WATER
PRIBADI/ DILARANG MASUK	_pribadee/ dilarang/ masuk_	PRIVATE/KEEP OUT
TANDA MEBAKARAN	_tanda cebacaran_	FIRE ALARM
DILARANG MEMBUANG SAMPAH	_dilarang membuang sampa_	NO LITTER
HATI-HATI	_hatee-hatee_	MIND THE STEP
CAT BASAH	_chat basa_	WET PAINT
KELAS SATU	_cerlas satoo_	FIRST CLASS (train)
KELAS DUA	_cerlas dua_	SECOND CLASS (train)

Road signs

STOP	*stop*	STOP
PELAN-PELAN	*per<u>lan</u> per<u>lan</u>*	SLOW
TETAP DI JALUR KANAN	*ter<u>tap</u> dee <u>ja</u>lur <u>ca</u>nan*	KEEP RIGHT
TETAP DI JALUR KIRI	*ter<u>tap</u> dee <u>ja</u>lur <u>ci</u>ree*	KEEP LEFT
SATU ARAH	*<u>sa</u>too <u>a</u>ra*	ONE WAY
DILARANG MENDAHULUI	*di<u>la</u>rang mernda<u>hu</u>luee*	NO PASSING [OVERTAKING]
DILARANG PARKIR	*di<u>la</u>rang <u>par</u>cir*	NO PARKING
JALAN BEBAS HAMBATAN	*<u>ja</u>lan <u>be</u>bas hamba<u>tan</u>*	HIGHWAY [MOTORWAY]
TOL	*tol*	TOLL
LAMPU LALU LINTAS	*<u>lam</u>poo <u>la</u>loo <u>lin</u>tas*	TRAFFIC LIGHTS
PEREMPATAN	*perrermpa<u>tan</u>*	INTERSECTION [JUNCTION]

Airport/Station

INFORMASI	*informasee*	INFORMATION
PERON 1	*perron satoo*	PLATFORM 1
PINTU 1	*pintoo satoo*	GATE 1
BEA CUKAI	*bea chucay*	CUSTOMS
IMIGRASI	*imigrasee*	IMMIGRATION
KEDATANGAN	*cerdatangan*	ARRIVALS
KEBERANGKATAN	*cerberrangcatan*	DEPARTURES
PENITIPAN BARANG	*pernitipan barang*	LUGGAGE LOCKERS
PENGAMBILAN BARANG	*perngambilan barang*	BAGGAGE [RE]CLAIM
BIS	*bis*	BUS
KERETA API	*cerreta apee*	TRAIN
SEWA MOBIL	*sewa mobil*	CAR RENTAL

Hotel/Restaurant

INFORMASI	*informasee*	INFORMATION
PENERIMAAN TAMU	*pernerrimaan tamoo*	RECEPTION
SUDAH DIPESAN	*suda dipesan*	RESERVED
DARURAT/PINTU KEBAKARAN	*darurat/pintoo cerbacaran*	EMERGENCY/ FIRE EXIT
AIR PANAS	*air panas*	HOT (WATER)
AIR DINGIN	*air dingin*	COLD (WATER)
KHUSUS PEGAWAI	*khusus pergaway*	STAFF ONLY
DILARANG MEROKOK	*dilarang merrocok*	NO SMOKING
PENITIPAN	*pernitipan*	COATCHECK [CLOAKROOM]
KOLAM RENANG	*colam rernang*	SWIMMING POOL
TERAS/TAMAN	*terras/taman*	TERRACE/GARDEN
BAR	*bar*	BAR

Stores

BUKA	_buca_	OPEN
TUTUP	_tutup_	CLOSED
MAKAN SIANG	_macan siang_	LUNCH
BAGIAN	_bagian_	DEPARTMENT
LANTAI	_lantay_	FLOOR
BAWAH TANAH	_bawa tana_	BASEMENT
LIFT	_lift_	ELEVATOR [LIFT]
TANGGA BERJALAN	_tangga berjalan_	ESCALATOR
KASIR	_casir_	CASHIER
OBRAL	_obral_	SALE

Sightseeing

BEBAS MASUK	*bebas masuk*	FREE ADMISSION
DEWASA	*dewasa*	ADULTS
ANAK-ANAK	*anak anak*	CHILDREN
TARIFKHUSUS (PELAJAR/MANULA)	*tarif khusus*	CONCESSIONS (students/ senior citizens)
CENDERAMATA	*chenderramata*	SOUVENIRS
MINUMAN/ MAKANAN RINGAN	*minuman/ macanan ringan*	REFRESHMENTS
JANGAN PEGANG	*jagang pergang*	DO NOT TOUCH
DILARANG MEMOTRET	*dilarang mermotret*	NO PHOTOGRAPHY
HARAP ENANG	*harap ternang*	SILENCE
TAK ADA JALAN KELUAR	*tak ada jalan cerluar*	NO ACCESS

Public Buildings

RUMAH SAKIT	*ruma sacit*	HOSPITAL
DOKTER	*docter*	DOCTOR
DOKTER GIGI	*docter gigee*	DENTIST
POLISI	*polisee*	POLICE
BANK	*bank*	BANK
KANTOR POS	*cantor pos*	POST OFFICE
KOLAM RENANG	*colam rernang*	SWIMMING POOL
BALAI KOTA	*balay cota*	TOWN HALL
ANTRI TAKSI	*antree tacsee*	TAXI STAND [RANK]
APOTEK	*apotek*	PHARMACY
KOLAM RENANG UMUM	*colam rernang umum*	PUBLIC SWIMMING POOL
MUSEUM	*museum*	MUSEUM

Reference

Numbers Nomor-nomor

0 **nol** *nol*

1 **satu** *satoo*

2 **dua** *dua*

3 **tiga** *tiga*

4 **empat** *ermpat*

5 **lima** *lima*

6 **enam** *ernam*

7 **tujuh** *tuju*

8 **delapan** *derlapan*

9 **sembilan** *sermbilan*

10 **sepuluh** *serpulu*

11 **sebelas** *serberlas*

12 **duabelas** *duaberlas*

13 **tigabelas** *tigaberlas*

14 **empatbelas** *ermpatberlas*

15 **limabelas** *limaberlas*

16 **enambelas** *ernamberlas*

17 **tujuhbelas** *tujuberlas*

18 **delapanbelas**
    derlapanberlas

19 **sembilanbelas**
    sermbilanberlas

20 **duapuluh** *duapulu*

21 **duapuluh satu**
    duapulu satoo

22 **duapuluh dua** *duapulu dua*

23 **duapuluh tiga** *duapulu tiga*

24 **duapuluh empat**
    duapulu ermpat

25 **duapuluh lima**
    duapulu lima

26 **duapuluh enam**
    duapulu ernam

27 **duapuluh tujuh** *duapulu tuju*

28 **duapuluh delapan**
    duapulu derlapan

29 **duapuluh sembilan**
    duapulu sermbilan

30 **tigapuluh** *tigapulu*

31 **tigapuluh satu**
    tigapulu satoo

32 **tigapuluh dua** *tigapulu dua*

40 **empat puluh** *ermpatpulu*

50 **limapuluh** *limapulu*

60	**enampuluh** *ernampulu*	a half	**setengah** *sertenga*
70	**tujuhpuluh** *tujupulu*	half an hour	**setengah jam** *sertenga jam*
80	**delapanpuluh** *derlapanpulu*	half a tank	**setengah tangki** *sertenga tangcee*
90	**sembilanpuluh** *sermbilanpulu*	half eaten	**setengah habis** *sertenga habis*
100	**seratus** *serratus*	a quarter	**seperempat** *serperrermpat*
101	**seratus satu** *serratus satoo*	a third	**sepertiga** *serpertiga*
102	**seratus dua** *serratus dua*	a pair of …	**sepasang …** *serpasang*
200	**dua ratus** *dua ratus*	a dozen …	**selusin …** *serlusin*
500	**lima ratus** *lima ratus*		
1,000	**seribu** *serriboo*	1999	**seribu sembilan ratus sembilanpuluh sembilan** *serriboo sermbilan ratus sermbilanpulu sembilan*
10,000	**sepuluh ribu** *serpulu riboo*		
35,750	**tigapuluh lima ribu tujuh ratus limapuluh** *tigapulu lima tuju ratus limapulu*	the 1990s	**seribu sembilan ratus sembilan puluhan** *serriboo sermbilan ratus sermbilan puluhan*
1,000,000	**satu juta** *satoo juta*		
first	**pertama** *pertama*	the year 2000	**tahun dua ribu** *tahun dua riboo*
second	**kedua** *cerdua*	2001	**dua ribu satu** *dua riboo satoo*
third	**ketiga** *certiga*		
fourth	**keermpat** *cerermpat*	2002	**dua ribu dua** *dua riboo dua*
fifth	**kelima** *cerlima*		
once	**sekali** *sercalee*	2003	**dua ribu tiga** *dua riboo tiga*
twice	**dua kali** *dua calee*		
three times	**tiga kali** *tiga calee*		

Days Hari-hari

Monday	**Senin** *sernin*
Tuesday	**Selasa** *serlasa*
Wednesday	**Rabu** *raboo*
Thursday	**Kamis** *camis*
Friday	**Jum'at** *juma'at*
Saturday	**Sabtu** *sabtoo*
Sunday	**Minggu** *minggoo*

Months Bulan-bulan

January	**Januari** *januaree*
February	**Februari** *februaree*
March	**Maret** *maret*
April	**April** *april*
May	**Mei** *mei*
June	**Juni** *junee*
July	**Juli** *julee*
August	**Agustus** *agustus*
September	**September** *september*
October	**Oktober** *october*
November	**November** *november*
December	**Desember** *desember*

Dates Tanggal-tanggal

It's …	**Pada …** *pada*
July 10	**tanggal sepuluh Juli**
	tanggal serpulu julee
Tuesday, March 1	**hari Selasa, tanggal satu Maret**
	haree serlasa, tanggal satoo maret
yesterday	**kemarin** *cermarin*
today/tomorrow	**hari ini/besok** *haree inee/besok*
this/last/next	**ini/lalu/depan** *inee/laloo/derpan*
every	**setiap** *sertiap*
week/month/year	**minggu/bulan/tahun**
	minggoo/bulan/tahun
on [at] the weekend	**pada akhir minggu**
	pada akhir minggoo

Seasons Musim-musim

spring	**musim semi** _musim sermee_
summer	**musim panas** _musim panas_
fall [autumn]	**musim gugur** _musim gugur_
winter	**musim dingin** _musim dingin_
in spring	**pada musim semi** _pada musim sermee_
during the summer	**selama musim panas** _serlama musim panas_

Greetings Ucapan-ucapan

Happy birthday!	**Selamat ulang tahun!** _serlamat oolang tahun_
Happy New Year!	**Selamat Tahun Baru!** _serlamat tahun baroo_
Congratulations!	**Selamat!** _serlamat_
Good luck!/All the best!	**Semoga Berhasil!** _sermoga berhasil_
Give my regards to …	**Salam untuk …** _salam untuk_

Public holidays Hari libur nasional

25th December	**Hari Natal**	Christmas Day
1st January	**Tahun Baru**	New Year's Day
17 August	**Kemerdekaan**	Independence Day
Movable dates:		
	Idul Adha	Muslim Holy Day
	Jum'at Agung	Good Friday
	Paskah	Easter
	Lebaran	Muslim Holy Day
	Nyepi	Seclusion day
	Waisak	Birthday anniversary of Buddha
	Maulud Nabi	Birthday of the Prophet Mohammed

Time Waktu

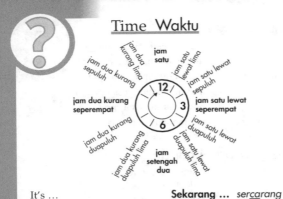

jam dua kurang lima
jam dua kurang sepuluh
jam satu
jam satu lewat lima
jam satu lewat sepuluh
jam dua kurang seperempat
jam satu lewat seperempat
jam dua kurang duapuluh
jam satu lewat duapuluh
jam dua kurang duapuluh lima
jam satu lewat duapuluh lima
jam setengah dua

It's …	**Sekarang …** *sercarang*
five past one	**jam satu lewat lima**
	jam satoo lewat lima
ten past two	**jam dua lewat sepuluh**
	jam dua lewat serpulu
a quarter past three	**jam tiga lewat seperempat**
	jam tiga lewat serperermpat
twenty past four	**jam empat lewat duapuluh**
	jam ermpat lewat duapulu
twenty-five past five	**jam lima lewat duapuluh lima**
	jam lima lewat duapulu lima
half past six	**jam setengah tujuh**
	jam sertenga tuju
twenty-five to seven	**jam tujuh kurang duapuluh lima**
	jam tuju curang duapulu lima
twenty to eight	**jam delapan kurang duapuluh**
	jam derlapan curang duapulu
a quarter to nine	**jam sembilan kurang seperempat**
	jam sermbilan curang serperempat
ten to ten	**jam sepuluh kurang sepuluh**
	jam serpulu curang serpulu
five to eleven	**jam sebelas kurang lima**
	jam serbelas curang lima
twelve o'clock	**jam dua belas** *jam duaberlas*

in the morning	**pada pagi hari** *pada pagee haree*
before lunch	**sebelum makan siang** *serbelum macan siang*
after lunch	**sesudah makan siang** *sersudah macan siang*
in the afternoon	**pada siang hari** *pada siang haree*
in the evening	**pada sore hari** *pada sore haree*
at night	**pada malam hari** *pada malam haree*
I'll be ready in five minutes.	**Saya akan siap dalam waktu lima menit.** *saya acan siap dalam wactoo lima mernit*
He'll be back in a quarter of an hour.	**Dia akan kembali dalam waktu seperempat jam.** *dia acan cermbalee dalam wactoo serperrermpat jam*
She arrived half an hour ago.	**Dia sampai setengah jam yang lalu.** *dia sampay sertenga jam yang laloo*
The train leaves at …	**Kereta api berangkat jam …** *cerreta apee berrangcat jam*
13:04	**tigabelas kosong empat** *tigabelas cosong ermpat*
00:40	**kosong kosong empatpuluh** *cosong cosong ermpatpulu*
The train is 10 minutes late/early.	**Kereta api terlambat/terlalu cepat sepuluh mernit.** *cerreta apee terlambat/ terlaloo cherpat serpulu mernit*
It's 5 minutes fast/slow.	**Itu lebih cepat/pelan lima menit.** *itoo lebi cherpat/perlan lima mernit*
from 9:00 a.m. to 5:00 p.m.	**dari jam sembilan pagi sampai jam lima sore** *daree jam sermbilan pagee sampay lima sore*
between 8:00 and 2:00	**antara jam delapan dan jam dua** *antara jam derlapan dan jam dua*
I'll be leaving by …	**Saya akan berangkat pada …** *saya acan berrangcat pada*

221

PHILIPPINE SEA

Philippines

CELEBES SEA

Manado ○

Moluccas

○ Palu

Sulawesi

Jayapura ○

Irian Jaya

Ujung Pandang ○

New Guinea

n e s i a

Flores

BANDA SEA

Sumba   **Timor**

Kupang

ARAFURA SEA

TIMOR SEA

Australia

Quick reference Petunjuk kilat

Good morning.	**Selamat pagi.** *serlamat pagee*
Good afternoon.	**Selamat siang.** *serlamat siang*
Good evening.	**Selamat sore.** *serlamat sore*
Hello.	**Halo.** *halo*
Good-bye.	**Sampai jumpa.** *sampay jumpa*
Excuse me! (*getting attention*)	**Permisi!** *permisee*
Sorry!	**Maaf!** *ma'af*
Please.	**Tolong.** *tolong*
Thank you.	**Terima kasih.** *terrima casee*
Do you speak English?	**Apa anda berbicara bahasa Inggris?** *apa anda berbichara bahasa inggris*
I don't understand.	**Saya tidak mengerti.** *saya tidak merngertee*
Where's …?	**Dimana …?** *dimana …*
Where are the restrooms [toilets]?	**Dimana kamar kecil?** *dimana camar cechil*

Emergency Keadaan darurat

Help!	**Tolong!** *tolong*
Go away!	**Pergi !** *pergee*
Call the police!	**Panggil polisi!** *panggil polisee*
Stop thief!	**Setop Maling!** *sertop maling*
Get a doctor!	**Panggilkan dokter!** *panggilcan docter*
Fire!	**Kebakaran!** *cebacaran*
I'm ill.	**Saya sakit** *saya sacit*
I'm lost.	**Saya kesasar.** *saya cersasar*
Can you help me?	**Bisa anda menolong saya?** *bisa anda mernolong saya*

Fire ☎ 110	Police ☎ 113	Ambulance ☎ 118

Embassies/Consulates

Australia	522.7111	U.K.	390.7484
Canada	525.0709	U.S.A.	344.2211